The
Romance of the Rose
or
Guillaume de Dole

University of Pennsylvania Press
MIDDLE AGES SERIES
Edited by
Edward Peters
Henry Charles Lea Professor
of Medieval History
University of Pennsylvania

A listing of the available books
in the series appears at the
back of this volume

The
Romance of the Rose
or
Guillaume de Dole

by Jean Renart

Translated, with an Introduction
by Patricia Terry and Nancy Vine Durling

University of Pennsylvania Press

Philadelphia

Copyright © 1993 by the University of Pennsylvania Press
All rights reserved
Printed in the United States of America

Library of Congress Cataloging-in-Publication Data to come

Jean Renart, 12/13th cent.
  [Roman de la Rose. English]
  The romance of the rose, or, Guillaume de Dole / by Jean Renart ; translated, with an
introduction by Patricia Terry and Nancy Vine Durling.
     p.   cm. — (Middle Ages series)
  Includes bibliographical references and index.
  ISBN 0-8122-3111-2. — ISBN 0-8122-1388-2 (pbk.)
     1. Romances—Translations into English.   I. Title: Romance of the rose.   II. Title:
Guillaume de Dole.   III. Series.
PQ1486.J7G8513   1993
841'.1—dc20   92-16414
                                                                              CIP

Contents

Acknowledgments

We are particularly happy to have this opportunity to thank Jeanette Beer, who introduced us to each other at the first Purdue Conference on Languages, Literatures, and Film in 1989. She has provided a greatly appreciated forum for students of medieval translation, and for the translation of medieval texts.

Our translation has greatly benefited from the work of French scholars, chief among them Jean Dufournet.

We wish to thank Patricia Stirnemann of the Bibliothèque Nationale, Paris for her valuable suggestions.

We would like to express our appreciation to Florida Atlantic University, which provided course relief for Professor Durling.

We want to express our appreciation to Robert M. Durling for his help with discordant computers.

The translators are grateful to each other for long patience and forebearance, and to their husbands for the same.

Introduction

A Preliminary Note

Little is known of the early thirteenth-century writer Jean Renart. Only three works have been attributed to him with any degree of certainty: a romance called *L'Escoufle* (*The Kite*), a short narrative poem called *Le Lai de l'Ombre* (*The Reflection*), and *Le Roman de la Rose* (*The Romance of the Rose*, or, *Guillaume de Dole*).[1] Dates given for *The Romance of the Rose* range from 1204 to 1228, although recent research has offered compelling evidence for the earlier date.[2] *Guillaume de Dole* is a subtitle added by a seventeenth-century critic in order to avoid confusion with the better known *Romance of the Rose* written by Guillaume de Lorris ca. 1225 and completed by Jean de Meun ca. 1270.[3]

The term "romance" refers to a type of narrative made popular in France in the early twelfth century with the development of vernacular literature. The first writers of romance borrowed themes and characters from classical antiquity; to these they added vivid descriptions of love relationships, reflecting contemporary enthusiasm for the work of Ovid, and drawing on the nascent literature of the southern love poets, the troubadours.[4] Twelfth-century romances were written in octosyllabic couplets, which remained the normal medium for fictional narratives until literary prose developed in the thirteenth century. The most celebrated writer of medieval romance, Chrétien de Troyes (flourished 1165–1190), replaced Greece and Rome with the court of King Arthur. His successor, Jean Renart, preferred vividly depicted realistic settings, an orientation that came to dominate later romances. These later, "realistic" romances richly convey the details of everyday life in the early thirteenth century. Jean Renart is arguably the most accomplished practitioner of this type of romance.

Jean Renart himself does not hesitate to make large claims for his works. *Guillaume de Dole* in particular shows a noteworthy pride of authorship. In his preface he lays claim to a striking innovation: he will include in the story a considerable number of lyric poems, some of them informal and anonymous, others by well-known troubadours and *trouvères*, poets from northern France. His work, he claims, will be so skillfully executed that the reader will think that the author himself has composed the poems to fit the fictional occasion. Jean Renart's work is indeed the first extant example of the combined use of narrative and lyric in French; as such, it has been of particular interest to historians of music.[5] A wide variety of musical genres are represented, ranging from the *chansons de toile*, or spinning songs, to courtly lyrics. Musical notation for the songs is not, however, included in the single extant manuscript of the work, which usually gives only one or two stanzas of a poem.[6] Félix Lecoy, the most recent editor of the romance, has consulted contemporary *chansonniers* (song books) in order to provide, when possible, missing lines. We have followed Lecoy's edition throughout; any departures have been indicated in the notes. Our translation aspires to suggest, rather than to duplicate, the rigorously defined fixed forms of the courtly lyric.[7] Other aspects of the translation are discussed below.

When Guillaume de Dole's sister Liénor arrives at the Emperor Conrad's court, people say she looks like the maidens who used to visit the fabled court of King Arthur. That imaginary kingdom has never lost its glamour. In the reference to it we "recognize" Liénor's extraordinary beauty and the fictive landscape to which it seems to belong. But the reference also distinguishes Liénor from the ladies of Camelot, and in the momentary gleam of Chrétien de Troyes' Celtic magic we may see her more clearly than in Jean Renart's more shifting, natural light. Similarly, tournaments in Chrétien's romances may strike us as less fantastic than the realistic events in *Guillaume de Dole* where a literary protagonist fights among actual people. Although irony pervades the work of both authors, Chrétien's is never aggressive; it creates a sense of complicity with the reader. The object of Jean Renart's irony may be ourselves, taken in, like the victims of Renard the Fox, by a persuasive story. But, unlike those victims, we never quite find out.

In the prologue to *Guillaume de Dole* Jean Renart tells us that the book will win him renown because it not only incorporates lyric poems but does so in such a skillful way that we believe the narrator of the romance to be the poet. This striking remark can be understood as anything from a mild pleasantry to a clue about how we should orient our reading; it hints, in any case, at artistic deception, a major theme in the work. The importance of fiction-making in the story is introduced by the minstrel, Jouglet, when he tells what he claims is a true story.[8] In it he describes a lady's beauty, and the narrator praises his skill. But the story *is* fiction, assumed to be so by the emperor to whom it is told, and known to be so by readers who recognize characters out of another work by Jean Renart. The skill is thus doubly that of the author, whose minstrel proceeds to another narration, this one about "real" people who live in the very country where all these stories are being told.

Although later writers imitated Jean Renart by introducing songs into their romances, they did not weave his complex connections between writer and reader, singers and their songs, fiction and fictional reality. It is not surprising that the unreliability of appearances is another central theme in Jean Renart's works. In his earliest romance, *L'Escoufle*, a misleading appearance is a key element in the development of the plot; judgment from insufficient evidence becomes the source of endless difficulties for the protagonists. In *Le Lai de l'Ombre*, evaluation of appearances is the plot itself: a lady, courted by a knight she finds attractive, cannot be sure of the sentiments that his words claim to represent. She is ultimately convinced by gesture rather than language, inspiration rather than intelligence.

In *Guillaume de Dole* there are characters who lie and credulous listeners, the reader perhaps among them. The narrative is constantly undermined by the way in which it is told; we begin to wonder what the story *is*. Our individual interpretations become part of the very structure of the text.

The plot of *Guillaume de Dole* is, or seems to be, as follows. The Emperor Conrad, the best and most charming of rulers, has only one defect: he enjoys his life so much he has no desire to settle down and get married. One day, however, his favorite minstrel tells him a story about a valiant knight and a lady of extraordinary beauty. Conrad laments that no such people are to be found in real life, but Jouglet replies that an even more exceptional knight and lady, Guillaume de Dole and his sister Liénor, are living in Conrad's own kingdom. The description of the lady and, more than anything else, the sound of the name Liénor cause Conrad to fall in love. He sends for Guillaume, who soon distinguishes himself by his personal charm and his skill in tournament fighting. Conrad confides to Guillaume his desire to marry Liénor, despite the difference in their rank.

But Conrad's seneschal becomes aware of this plan, and, jealous of Guillaume's increasing power at court, finds a way to prevent the marriage. He goes in secret to Guillaume's house. He is not allowed to see Liénor herself, sequestered when her brother is absent, but he learns from her mother, to whom he gives a valuable ring, that the maiden has a distinguishing mark, a rose, on her thigh. With this information he persuades the emperor that his beloved is no longer a virgin. The seneschal claims to have seduced her himself, and his knowledge of the rose is convincing evidence. Conrad, in great distress, tells this to Guillaume. The failure of the marriage is so disappointing to the knight that he falls ill. A nephew learns what has happened and rushes off, sword in hand, to accuse Liénor of disgracing the family. Her mother realizes the harm she has done by her ill-advised talk.

Liénor travels to court to conduct her own defense. She sends a messenger to the seneschal with gifts purporting to be from a certain lady, a token that she has decided to grant him her love. He is to wear the belt and jewels under his clothes. Liénor appears before the emperor, who of course does not know who she is, and accuses the seneschal of both rape and theft; the belt and jewels are impressive evidence. The seneschal, knowing himself to be innocent of these crimes, asks for a trial by ordeal. When this proves him innocent, Liénor turns his triumph against him, revealing her identity and the way he had tried to destroy her reputation. Only by Liénor's mercy does the seneschal escape death. He is exiled in disgrace, and the marriage of Conrad and Liénor is joyfully celebrated.

The first hint that this outline of the plot may be inadequate occurs when the emperor is described: the best and most admirable of rulers, "he hated wickedness and dining in front of a fire in summertime." This is hardly the juxtaposition we might have expected. In the same passage we read that Conrad was worth "a whole bushel basket full of the kings who came after him," which doesn't do much for their prestige or his own. And, a few lines further on, we are told that Conrad, as judge, could not be influenced even by a bribe of a thousand marks, a large sum, but not infinitely large.

The spirit in which we are to take such remarks, sprinkled like salt over the text, is uncertain. They seldom call attention to themselves, but are just insistent enough to create an uneasy feeling. We retain an impression of Conrad that prevents our taking him quite seriously as a ruler. This may be a quality in itself, part of his undeniable charm; it may, however, cast doubt on the quality of his love for Liénor, which is based entirely on hearsay.

Jouglet's initial description of Guillaume de Dole, a paragon among knights, includes the information that he is not really entitled to his name: he doesn't come from Dole but from a less impressive village nearby. Wanting to give himself an appearance of distinction is, according to Jouglet, simply good sense on Guillaume's part. The emperor agrees and instantly changes the subject.

But Guillaume's name is often underlined by the pun, available to some extent in English, that makes him guileful. The possibilities of *dole* in English, in addition to the "doleful" of which Jean Renart is so fond, include the very appropriate "on the dole." Guillaume does certainly live beyond his means, but this again may be regarded either as the good fortune of having rich friends to further one's commendable ambitions, or as a kind of dishonesty. Old French *doleusement* implies ruse and fraud.

Liénor's name is particularly rich in "hidden" meanings. It combines *lien* (link; *lié*: linked) and *or* (gold), which can refer to her hair, constantly praised for its gold color. The name, often juxtaposed with a reference to *or*, underscores her value as a beauty and potential bride; but it may also suggest the wealth she does not possess. The noun *li enors* means honor in Old French, whereas the adjective *lié* means joyful, in opposition to *dole*, sorrow. The Old French form of the emperor's name, Corras, has a syllable of gold, possibly a link with Liénor, although he was inexhaustibly rich. The name suggests physicality: *cors* (body); and *cuers* (heart).[9]

Critics have differed greatly in their reactions to these complexities in the text. Rita Lejeune, discussing the description of Conrad, sees only a positive connection between hating sin and appropriate dining conditions: the emperor loved virtue *and* the good life. She sees nothing suggestive in the names of any of the characters, mentions no double meanings. For her the plot is just as we have outlined it above, although she notes in passing that Guillaume greets Jouglet as an old friend, addressing him with surprising familiarity.

Michel Zink, author of the first book on *Guillaume de Dole*, does not take the apparent plot for the meaning. Everything happens too easily. The seneschal, without even a plan in mind, extracts an intimate secret from Liénor's mother. Liénor reestablishes her reputation by means of improbable knowledge of the seneschal's own secrets, and by his unforeseeable insistence on a trial by ordeal. An implicit contrast is thus established between literature and reality, to the advantage of the former.

Zink argues that Conrad's love for Liénor, sight unseen, is convincing only as fiction. It has literary, not psychological, precedents, in particular the love of the troubadour Jaufré Rudel for the unknown Lady of Tripoli. Like love, wealth becomes a fictional construct; money circulates so freely in Conrad's kingdom that no one really pays for anything. Similarly, the presence of real people in a literary setting reminds us that the setting is *not* real.

While Lejeune places the date of *Guillaume de Dole* close to 1212, Zink follows Félix Lecoy in preferring 1228. In that case, Guillaume de Lorris's *Roman de la Rose* may have preceded it. Whatever the true chronological order, the difference in the way the two works use the same symbol points to the literary emphasis of Jean Renart. Guillaume de Lorris's rose is a sexual organ; in Jean Renart it is a way of referring to sexuality. The rose is constantly associated with speech, notably in the strange statement of Liénor's mother that no one *qui parler puisse* (literally, "who is capable of speech") will ever see such a marvel. That the rose refers specifically to Liénor's virginity is indicated by the often recurring euphemism *chose* (thing), again a manner of speaking. The meaning of the text, Zink tells us, is to be found not in its depths but on its surface; the author is ever-present but only in the form of a smile, like that of the Cheshire Cat.

The Freudian critic Henri Rey-Flaud also sees Jean Renart's work as a response to that of Guillaume de Lorris, but understands Liénor's mother's statement, quoted above, to mean that the rose signifies the unattainable. Conrad falls in love with the name of a woman, with her *sign*, *Liénor*; the rest of her name, *Dole*, and that of her brother, *Guillaume*, would allude to the deceptiveness of his quest for a corresponding reality. Rey-Flaud also suggests that when the seneschal is searched, and female sexual symbols, the jewels and the purse, are found on his body, an inversion of rôles occurs: he is victimized by Liénor, while she takes his place manipulating Conrad.

If only in this last point, Rey-Flaud agrees with Roger Dragonetti, for whom *Guillaume de Dole* is all about manipulation. As Dragonetti reads it, Guillaume, Liénor, and their mother are conspirators whose intention is simply to rise in the world. He notes that their home is twice referred to as a *repaire*, which can also mean a den or lair, like the one occupied by Renart the Fox. Dragonetti emphasizes the love of Guillaume for his sister, ex-pressed in terms much more eloquent than any used by Conrad.

Jouglet is the conspirators' indispensable ally. His is the seductive power of literature, of song, through which empty hyperbole acquires magical power. But the central figure, in this reading, is the mother. It is she who directs and informs the "guile" of her son. Far from being naive, she deliberately gives the seneschal the means of destroying the marriage proj-ect, in order to guarantee its success in the future.

It is here that we would find the principal difficulty with Dragonetti's interpretation. The mother would have understood the seneschal's pur-poses and known exactly how they would be turned against him. That was why, for example, she refused to allow him to see Liénor, who would have to be incognito when she went to court. Unless the mother was actually a witch, this much foreknowledge seems most unlikely.

There remains, however, the possibility that she told the seneschal about the rose simply to enhance her daughter's value in the eyes of an influential person at court. Had the seneschal related it to Conrad simply as hearsay, the rose might well have been an asset to Liénor, strange and suggestive. The impressive ring could have been an indication to the mother that the seneschal was disposed in their favor; it need not be seen as a bribe. It is clear that she thought her daughter worthy of being an empress, even destined to be one. But hopes and dreams are not a conspiracy. We ourselves are inclined to see the plotting as limited to Guillaume and Jouglet. When Jouglet comes to meet Guillaume at his inn, their conversation is most easily explained by a prior complicity: Jouglet is reporting on how he has proceeded to carry out their plan. As the first step, Conrad had to invite the young knight to court. When Guillaume dines with the emperor, Jouglet steers the conversation toward the tournament where Guillaume will have a chance to show off his skills. This is essential if a marriage between an emperor and a girl of much lower rank is to be accomplished. Guillaume's despair at the loss of these hopes has a very personal tone: he believes his position at court to be dependent on that of his sister.

There seems to us no evidence that either Liénor or her mother was a participant in these arrangements, although they were possibly aware of them. In any case, whatever conspiracy there may have been, it comes to nothing, and Liénor alone must reestablish her good name and her future. Her instantaneous creation of an elaborate plot suggests a power of mind that could fairly be called formidable, even unscrupulous, although we would not go so far as Dragonetti's "diabolical."

Gossip being what it is in all times and places, Liénor could have known about the seneschal's unrequited love, and there seems nothing problematical in her trying to look her best when she appears at court, even if the author so carefully describes her décolletage. Her arguments before the court follow strict legal formalities, and the difficulty of proving a negative fact is very well known. But although planting evidence on a guilty person may be the only way to bring about justice, in moral terms it is scarcely the method of choice. The distress of the seneschal's friends is so great that Liénor herself wonders, for a moment, if she has committed a sin. In any event, she is totally successful.

The depiction of Liénor's resourceful intelligence is something quite new in medieval literature. Chrétien de Troyes' Enide shows herself capable of independent and effective action, Marie de France's Guildeluec is an example of extraordinary compassion, Iseut is a queen and a healer. But, like other strong women in twelfth- and thirteenth-century romance, they are seen in the context of a love relationship that determines their behavior. Liénor is primarily concerned to reestablish her reputation and secure a crown. Her words to Conrad, "If I am destined to rule this kingdom, why should this unhappy creature be denied an honor she has done nothing to lose?" are political. There is never any mention of Liénor's feelings for Conrad; she expresses affection only for her mother and her brother.

Liénor's wedding robe is embroidered with scenes from the Trojan War. The story was well known to medieval audiences through Benoît de Sainte-Maure's *Roman de Troie*. There are two prior references to events at Troy, the first when Conrad is said to be "more valiant than anyone who fought there," the second when Guillaume, newly arrived at Conrad's court, is more welcome than anyone "since the time of the Trojan Paris." Furthermore, as Lejeune has pointed out, Nicole's description of Guillaume is an almost verbatim quotation from Benoît.[10] The wedding robe focuses primarily on the life of Helen; the description of her in *Le Roman de Troie* is also closely related to the description of Liénor.[11]

Thus each of the three major characters is specifically compared to a Trojan analogue, each time in a somewhat problematic way. Conrad's epic valor is immediately undermined by his dislike of "dining in front of a fire in summertime." Paris, however welcome, proves extremely treacherous to his royal host. The golden figure of Helen on the robe connects Liénor and Helen in their beauty and in its attendant dangers. The robe is the culmination of all the events of the story, and gives them a symbolic form which requires an ironic interpretation even as it glorifies love and beauty.

The interpolated songs embroidered on the text may also include ironic overtones in their celebration of love. These poems are drawn from a variety of traditions. They include verses by well-known troubadour and *trouvère* poets such as Jaufré Rudel and Gace Brulé, simple *caroles* or dance songs, *chansons de toile* or spinning songs, and even a fragment of epic. Of the major characters, Conrad sings the most, expressing a variety of moods and opinions. The first time, having just fallen in love, he evokes, with Jouglet, an exalted tradition: the lover's faithfulness and hope persist through the hardships of winter when all the birds are still. The inspiration for Conrad's second song is also his love for Liénor, but the setting is his sunlit bedroom where images of golden embroidered roses inspire thoughts of a more erotic nature.

After Guillaume arrives at court, the emperor returns to the theme of suffering in love, but with greater insistence. Specifically for Guillaume's pleasure is a song about the lover's constant thought of his beloved, the secret Conrad still has not revealed. When he finally does confide in Guillaume, a song further defines the lover's suffering; he becomes subservient to unworthy people because they have access to his beloved. The next song, overheard by the seneschal, is similar in theme, and inspires the plot to discredit Guillaume and Liénor. When Conrad has been convinced that she is unworthy, he sings the disadvantages of wanting to know too much. Later, he goes so far as to reproach Love itself for not rewarding his faithful service; in the following song, he reproaches himself for complaining. And finally, with Liénor in his arms, he sings that *her* joy must be absolute.

Guillaume, though he never sings alone, sings with others. He also asks Liénor to sing, and these are her only songs. When the emperor's messenger comes to invite Guillaume to court, he is allowed to visit Liénor and her mother in their apartments. There, among beautiful fabrics they have embroidered, they sing opposing songs: the mother's insists that Aude forget Doon. Liénor's first song seems to express the emotions of Aude, complaining of harsh treatment and vowing never to forget her love. In the second song Doette, rather than Aude, is waiting for Doon, but it doesn't seem that he will be coming. She, however, asserts the independence of her love. Liénor in this scene appears to be a reserved, well-brought-up young lady, but her songs argue a certain strong-mindedness.

Another song is placed in a sewing room, but the singer is a young man. Here a conversation between a mother and her unwed pregnant daughter comes to an unexpectedly happy conclusion. The charm of the song is what Zink considers the charm of the whole book: life is not like this at all. Yet our delight is in the contrast between "life" and "this," simultaneously evoked.

A song of particular interest is not a lyric poem but a fragment of an epic. It may have been written by Jean Renart himself, since Dragonetti's study of the sixty extant manuscripts of *Gerbert de Metz* failed to locate it. Although elements of the poem—the broken helmet, the royal gift of a horse, prisoners taken in battle—echo various aspects of the narrative, their significance is not clear. The most important contribution of this fragment seems to us its contrast with the whole world of romance. Its menacing warlike tone contrasts oddly with the rest of *Guillaume de Dole*, in which fighting is only a sport and prisoners taken for ransom are always freed. This is one of the longest poems, and the only one with no allusion to love. The relationships sketched are totally without courtly grace.

All these poems, according to the prologue, are said to color the text like red dye; within the epic tradition, the corresponding image would be the flowing of blood. Zink adds a more erotic interpretation: the red rose that gives the poem its title is a way of referring to the virginity Liénor is said to have lost. The rose ultimately becomes Liénor herself: "Je sui la pucele a la rose," she says to the emperor, "I am the maiden of the rose." Her phrase both separates and unites the promise of virginity and the distinctive rose. Conrad, however, remains in doubt until she identifies herself as the fair Liénor.

Then the emperor embraces what had been only the sound of a name, or the thought of a maiden equal to those who exist in books. The song which springs from his heart begins, "What more do you want, when I am yours?" both egocentric and honest, no doubt, from an emperor's point of view. Jean Renart succinctly expresses the basic reality: "Ahi! plus tire cus que corde," conservatively translated as "Sex pulls harder than a rope." With that the archbishop is sent to put on his ceremonial robes, and Liénor puts on hers.

Conrad's happiness on his wedding night is favorably compared to that of famous literary lovers. We are told nothing of Liénor on that occasion, except that she was not too badly injured to be fair-minded the next day. In *Erec et Enide* Chrétien is differently concerned about Enide's experience on her wedding night. Her consent is not taken for granted, her developing emotions are sensitively analyzed, and she participates equally with her husband. At a time when almost all marriages were arranged, Chrétien's is, no doubt, an idealizing vision, possibly intended to be instructive.

Liénor's rose, like her virginity, ceases to be important once the lineage is secure. She and her brother have high positions at court, a different court from the one to which they aspired, since Conrad has abandoned the carefree pastimes of his youth. The social and political realities of life will now become the whole, untold story.

Jean Renart dwells at some length on the political and economic aspects of Conrad's reign. This, as Lejeune points out, has no precedent among earlier writers of romance. His ideal ruler makes sure that only the nobles have power, and is particularly attentive to the lower nobility, the *vavasseurs*, for whom Jean Renart has a prediliction. But the peasants and bourgeois do well under Conrad's regime because he prefers not to tax them. This action is not magnanimity but self-interest: the gifts they offer him in return will be even more profitable, and their money remains available should he need it. In addition, Conrad takes care that merchants traveling through his kingdom are safe from bandits and thieves. Other aspects of the portrait of Conrad have been seen as a negative view of Philip Augustus, fond of instruments of war, including the prohibited crossbow, and indeed of war itself.[12]

Court life in *Guillaume de Dole* centers not so much on great deeds and serious love affairs as on splendid feasts and elaborate dress. The medieval love of luxury is fully shared by Jean Renart, who fills his narrative with ornate and colorful fabrics, elaborate furs, jewels, lavish gifts, and such an abundance of food and wines there could be nothing left to desire.

The guests at Conrad's summertime gatherings in the woods cared for singing and dancing more than they worried about their souls. Conrad is praised for spending money lavishly enough to be remembered after his death. Noble ladies and maidens come from miles around to participate in festivities that are far from prudish. All this has more of midsummer magic than of realistic description.

And yet there is a strange insistence on the opposition between the secular and the religious: birds are better than chaplains; the Bishop of Chartres would rather attend Conrad's dinner party than a synod; Guillaume's shields are carried like sacred relics; his men follow him in orderly pairs, like monks. In the last lines of the book its author hides the name Renart in the statement that he lost it when he took religious orders. He may, however, have lost his real name if he called himself Renart in homage to the Fox, whose word, as we are specifically reminded more than once in this text, was not to be trusted.

Conrad's guests at the *fête champêtre* are not individualized, except for being named as the singers of songs, and it is only in songs that they speak. Despite their lack of attention to religion, the elegantly dressed people who engage in music and love-making are clearly to be admired, at least in contrast to the large group of hunters. One wonders why these were invited, unless their wives were among the guests; they are, in fact, referred to as "jealous." The hunters kill any number of creatures, including foxes (again with a reference to Renard's adventures), and add much to the food supply, but inspire more mockery than gratitude. They eat by themselves, hungrier and cruder in their tastes than the others.

The sport which is taken most seriously in *Guillaume de Dole* is, of course, tournament fighting. It offers the only chance for Guillaume to compensate for his relatively low status. Jean Renart's literary purpose, like Chrétien's when he described a tournament, was to show the prowess of a particular hero. But, as Baldwin has shown, while Chrétien concentrates on individual jousts, Jean Renart follows Guillaume's activities without distorting the form of the tournament itself where opponents were not individuals but teams.[13] Those in front or on the sides of the tightly-knit groups would do the fighting, with the others as back-up. In *Guillaume de Dole* the only weapon is a long, heavy lance. A rich man would own a team of fighters, as now of football players, except that the owner might also be the captain. Team members would be paid a salary, but this might not compensate for their losses. Thus we see Saint-Trond being saved from looting only by Conrad's generous intervention.

Guillaume, who came with a group of his own, was not fighting for money, but the horses and weapons he captured, and the ransoms of prisoners, were a source of revenue. Baldwin sees his first three gifts as a payment of debts; his further generosity left him poorer than when he began, but rich in redeemable glory. Tournaments in other romances result in serious, even fatal wounds, but only Jean Renart shows us the minor cuts and bruises. His victorious hero returns to his inn exhausted and black-and-blue. Servants bring water to wash the grime from faces, and the festive mood is darkened by the presence of many who have had a discouraging day.

Readers of *Guillaume de Dole* in its own time would have recognized not only familiar features of the tournament but the participants themselves. Those named, according to Lejeune, would have been contemporaries of the poet, appropriately assigned either to the French or the German side. Even if a later date for *Guillaume de Dole* is correct, the names would have been in recent memory. Research can reestablish identities, but it cannot make them familiar. The modern reader might try to imagine a sporting event in a novel but with players familiar in real life.

Jean Renart tells us that the archbishop who married Conrad and Liénor wrote down the events which led to that ceremony in order to honor the participants, and especially to celebrate the protagonist's exemplary life. But there is no way to tell whether Jean Renart refers here to Guillaume or to Conrad. The added title *Guillaume de Dole* unfairly gives more importance to Guillaume. If, however, we think of his sister as his double, half of the ideal composite Jouglet described to the emperor, and taking the place Guillaume might have assumed in defense of her honor, we would have, if not the subject of the archbishop's chronicle, surely the true protagonist of this *Romance of the Rose*.

A Note on the Translation

The translation of the narrative portion of *Guillaume de Dole* presented a number of special problems. It is the unique source for a number of words—for details of dress and polite behavior—and proverbial expressions whose meaning can only be guessed. These are, as far as possible, glossed in the notes.

There are an exceptional number of personal and place names; names of historical characters are often intermingled with those of fictional ones. Our policy in translating the various names has been to use the French form (e.g., Guillaume de Dole), but to translate into English geographical names (the Count of Bar). Place names have been translated into English when they are identifiable; otherwise the French form is retained.

The text gives a vivid impression of courtly life, down to the dinner menus and white gloves on the ladies, and we value all its details. For this reason and, perhaps even more important, to protect Jean Renart's ambiguous irony so that readers of the translation could make their own assessment, we wanted to give a quite literal translation. We soon discovered, however, that the energy and momentum of rhymed couplets render unremarkable certain characteristics of medieval style that in prose seem either burdensome or quaint: the very frequent and redundant exclamations, arbitrary changes of tense, names of canonical hours. We have therefore standardized verb tenses throughout and, where appropriate, trimmed excessive repetition.

As an example of a more pervasive kind of difficulty, here is an ordinary sentence, which, literally translated, would read this way: "The lady and her daughter had dined with the very greatest delight." Superlatives are scattered so thickly through Old French texts that they have no chance to function by contrast. It can thus be argued that they don't function as superlatives at all, but are at most intensifiers, and often less significant than unqualified nouns. We quite readily become accustomed to this stylistic convention in Old French, but in English our best option is to translate superlatives according to what seems, as best we can tell, their actual effect. Our sample sentence might read "The lady and her daughter had enjoyed a very good dinner." Similarly, when the vassals of the Emperor Conrad lament his disinclination to take a wife, they say, "if he . . . dies without an heir, we are all dead . . . nothing will ever give us joy again," phrases for which reasonable equivalents might be "If he dies without an heir, we're lost . . . our happy days are over."

In other circumstances it has seemed that a more literal version, even if somewhat awkward, was the better option. A type of understatement that occurs from time to time in *Guillaume de Dole* owes more to the author's personal style than to conventions of the language. When we read that a messenger's horse was "neither sore nor lame" and he himself "neither a fool nor drunk," the phrases mean approximately that the horse was swift and the messenger well chosen for his task. But to give just this as a translation seems a reduction, a smoothing out of a perhaps intentional roughness. In such expressions, as also in the proverbs which refer to oxen, cabbages, goats, and herring, Jean Renart brings in aspects of unembellished reality that normally have no place in romance. A classical enumeration of Liénor's features concludes with the remark that her neck "par reson" had no sores or wrinkles. This isn't just an equivalent for the usual "her neck was white and smooth." "Par reson" means something like "of course," the "reason" being that Liénor was the heroine of a romance. The Old French words have adequate equivalents in English, but our version risks seeming more odd than effective. The author's phrase slips by in the charm of its rhyme: *sanz fronce/selon ce*. At another moment, Liénor is said to be neither a hunchback nor deformed. The description of Guillaume as he rides toward the tournament includes the information that his handsome face was not covered with blemishes.

The passage in which Guillaume and his sister are first named is especially significant, and rich in suggestions which cannot always be directly expressed in English. Old French *guile* rhymes with *vile*, meaning the village to whose name Guillaume was not entitled, plus a suggestion of the English "vile." In an English language version "Guillaume" and "guile" have a visual resemblance, but however "Guillaume" is pronounced there will be little guile in it. As for the heroine's name, the minstrel/author, by a rhyme, evokes Conrad's attraction to the unknown beauty, not idealizing but lustful: *cors* (body), Lié*nors*.

An adequate translation of this passage has to underline the reference to guile and give the king's words about Liénor a chance to express their sexual intention:

[Jouglet said,] "People there call him Guillaume de Dole, though he hasn't any right to the name."

"Then why does he use it?"

"Because he has a house nearby, and Dole sounds more impressive than just the name of the village. Using the name Dole shows good sense rather than guile."

"I think so, too," the emperor replied. "What is the name of his sister, who has such a fine and beautiful body?"

"Sire, I will tell you: her name is Liénor."

Notes

1. Dates for these works are still debated; it is usually agreed that they were written in the order indicated. Other works have been attributed to Jean Renart in the past. These include *Galeran de Bretagne* and two fabliaux.

2. See, e.g., the recent work by John Baldwin (1990).

3. The seventeenth-century critic is Claude Fauchet, cited by Servois, p. 1, as the first scholar to have called attention to the coincidence of names. Although Guillaume de Lorris's portion of *Le Roman de la Rose* was written at roughly the same time as Jean Renart's romance, it has never been possible to determine with certainty which work preceded the other. In any case, Jean de Meun's much longer continuation, in which many of the major debates of the thirteenth century are presented, became one of the most influential works of the Middle Ages. The title therefore was identified with the more famous work, and we follow the now established custom of referring to Jean Renart's romance as *Guillaume de Dole*.

4. These early romances are often referred to as *romans antiques*, or romances of antiquity. There is, however, debate among specialists concerning the genre of these early works, which differ markedly in subject matter from the works of such later writers as Chrétien de Troyes.

5. See, e.g., Coldwell and Page.

6. Vatican Reg. 1725, dating from the end of the thirteenth century.

7. A list of the songs and their first lines is appended. This information is also available in Lecoy's edition, pp. xxii–xxix. For a detailed discussion of the lyrics and music, see Coldwell and Page.

8. "Minstrel" is the usual translation of Old French *jongleur* (also called a *vïeleor*), a performer of songs and narratives who usually accompanied himself, or occasionally herself, on a vielle, a stringed instrument played with a bow, precursor of the violin.

9. A number of scholars have commented on the names *Liénor* and *Conrad*, among them Dragonetti, Durling, Kay, Rey-Flaud, Zink.

10. She cites the two passages in *Oeuvres*, p. 140.

11. For further discussion see Jung, pp. 37–38; 49–50. Jung makes the ingenious suggestion that Helen's name in Old French, which would be pronounced L N, combines with *or* to form Ellenore, of which Liénor is a variant.

12. See Lejeune, *Oeuvres*, pp. 65–68. Recent research by Baldwin tends to support this view, which had been somewhat discredited.

13. Baldwin, 1990, pp. 570–72.

The
Romance of the Rose
or
Guillaume de Dole

T he teller of this tale, who has included in it beautiful songs so that they may be remembered, hopes that his fame and renown will reach Rheims in Champagne and the ear of the handsome Milon de Nanteuil, one of the great men of our time. For just as one dyes cloth red to increase its worth, just so has he added poems and their melodies to this *Romance of the Rose*, which is something quite new.[1] It is so different from other works, being embroidered here and there with beautiful songs, that an uncouth person could never understand it. Believe me, this work surpasses all others. No one will ever tire of hearing it, because it can be both sung and read, and was composed with such great skill that it will seem endlessly new. It tells of fighting and love, and sings of them both at once. Everyone will imagine that the author of this romance also wrote the words of the songs, so well do they go with those of the story. Here begins the tale.

For many years, my lords, the Empire was ruled by Germans. And the story tells of an emperor who, like his father, was named Conrad. His people thought highly of him, and rightly so; I could tell of his virtues all day without doing him justice. There has never been his equal, even at Troy. He hated wickedness and dining in front of a fire in summertime.

Never in his life was he known to swear or to criticize anyone unfairly. He ruled through just decrees and laws, swayed by neither wealth nor poverty. He was wise and courtly by nature, and knew the joys of the chase better than anyone else in the world. He was worth a whole bushel basket full of the kings who came after him.

He fought with lance and shield, scorning the crossbow, unlike the highborn men of today in their greed and wickedness. Conrad wouldn't have used a crossbow to kill his worst enemy, not for half the treasure of Rome. On one half of the emperor's shield were the arms of the noble Count of Clermont; on the other, an azure lion rampant on a gold field.[2] Conrad in battle was fiercer than a leopard. But do you know what I like best about him? He was so fair-minded and so temperate in his habits that no one could ever accuse him of excess. He never stood on ceremony; his heart was genuinely noble, loving, and steadfast.

If a nobleman appealed to him for judgment in a case, he could be sure that even a thousand gold marks would not influence Conrad's decision. He wasn't easily moved to hatred, and loved nothing contrary to honor. When he heard of an old lord or a widowed lady living in poverty, he was quick to offer them clothes and anything else they needed. As for himself, he considered it wealth enough to have an abundance of knights around him, and he frequently rewarded them with jewels, silk clothing, and horses. At his court, which he held in both winter and summer, there was no end of knightly activity. Any good knight traveling through the empire was either persuaded to join his retinue or given land or castles appropriate to his rank.

The knights themselves were his only weapons of war. They carried his banners and lances into the fray; they took high towers and burned great castles to the ground. They didn't use machines; instead they hurled themselves against the besieged, and would have bitten through the walls with their bare teeth. Their lord had only to point out the fortresses to be taken. In such men resides a king's true treasure; thanks to them, Conrad's enemies were crushed and brought to their knees.

He did not yet have a wife, although his people were very eager to see him married. The noble lords often spoke of it together: "If this king—the best there has ever been—dies without an heir, we're lost!" They couldn't help remembering how they had all been brought up together, and how Conrad had showered them with honors and gifts; if he died childless, their happy days were over! For this reason they often broached with him the topic of marriage, but he wouldn't listen—the claims of youth were much more pressing.

In summertime, when it was pleasant to frolic in meadows and woods, he would have great tents set up. Everyone hurried out there from the cities to have a good time. Within three or four days' ride there wasn't a count or countess, a chatelaine, duchess, or lady who hadn't been sent for, nor a vassal within a seven-day ride. Conrad didn't care how much he spent as long as everything was done to his liking and would be talked about when he was dead and gone. He and his friends played delightful, elegant games, and he gave much thought to how each of them might find a sweetheart. Conrad himself, of course, without even trying, had no end of success. This good king was a very charming man and knew all the tricks of love.

At daybreak, archers came out of his tent to summon the hunters: "Arise, my lords! We're off to the woods!" You should have heard the horns blowing to wake up the knights! Conrad made sure that every lazy old man was presented with a bow. (No emperor, since the days of King Mark, has been better able to rid himself of bores.[3]) He would send spears and horns to those who were jealous and ill-natured, and then ride with them as far as the woods to make sure they didn't turn back. He asked some to serve as beaters with the archers. Others were ordered to follow the deerhounds. He kept them so well occupied that they were quite content. When they were deep in the forest enjoying themselves, Conrad and two of his boon companions would turn around and race straight back on an old carriage road, laughing all the way.

Meanwhile, the rest of the knights, exhausted from their exploits, were sleeping in silken tents beneath the elms. I really don't expect ever again to see people have such a wonderful time, nor so many ladies with pleated tunics tightly laced about their beautiful bodies and chaplets of gold and rubies on their wavy golden hair! Countesses wearing no cloaks were sheathed in samite and cloth-of-gold. There were maidens in cendal silk, whose chaplets were adorned with lovely birds and flowers. Their graceful bodies and firm little breasts were greatly admired. They wore fine slender belts and white gloves.[4] Singing sweetly, they would enter the rush-strewn tents where the knights were waiting to stretch out their arms and draw them under the covers. Anyone who has ever engaged in such sport knows what I'm talking about. They couldn't have cared less if the hunters stayed out all day! Their own pursuits were very different. The emperor arrived at a gallop and, bursting into a tent, shouted, "Well, knights, here's to the ladies!"[5]

They didn't worry much about their souls; there were neither bells nor churches (why would they need them?), nor chaplains except for the birds. They had everything they desired. God! They reclined on sumptuous quilt-covered beds singing beautiful songs and enjoying refined conversation. When the sun rose, they were already up and busy adorning themselves. Their tunics and cloaks of samite, imported cloth, or rich gold silk embroidered with birds, were beautifully trimmed with fine new furs: ermine, alternating bands of miniver, delicately scented black sable. Where would you find such elegance these days! The emperor, who didn't want to be better dressed than the others, wore a cloak trimmed with two bands of contrasting silk. And I'll tell you what improved the way it looked. With her own hands a maiden (bless her!) fastened his cloak with a pretty ribbon from her white shift and gave him a little white belt in exchange for his own. That valiant girl had better take good care of the emperor's belt, since even without the gold, the jewels made it very valuable. There were emeralds as green as ivy, worth a good forty marks. Long live Conrad!

By nine o'clock they were enjoying themselves out in the woods. Barefoot, their sleeves unsewn,[6] they came to a place, not far from the tents, where little islands had been formed by the water from springs. They gathered in small groups to wash their hands. The place was very attractive with its summery green foliage and abundance of little blue and white flowers. They washed their faces and then sewed up their sleeves. I think the maidens carried spools of thread in the little purses that hung from their belts. They didn't have any towels, but the ladies offered their white shifts, which gave many a man the chance to get his hands on a lovely white thigh. (Anyone who asked for more could hardly be called courtly!) In the meantime a meal was prepared and tablecloths spread. The ladies started back, along with the knights; not being shy, they were singing this little song[7]:

> I swear to God! if I can't get
> his love, I wish we'd never met.

One of the knights interrupted with:

> Under the branches bending low,
> that's the way true lovers should go,
>   bright are the flowing waters there.
>   Oh!
> So let him love whose lady's fair.

This song had hardly begun when a blond maiden, who had tucked up her exquisite tunic, started this one:

> And if my love's abandoned me,
> I will not die of that, you'll see!

But before she had finished it, a noble lady, the Duke of Mainz's sister, started to sing in a strong, pure voice:

> Lovely Aelis got up with the sun—
> sleep well, I pray you, jealous one—
> adorned and so prettily dressed,
>   where trees bend low,
> I see her come dancing along,
>   the one I love best.

Then the noble Count of Savoy sang this one:

> Lovely Aelis got up with the day,
> I see her come dancing along,
> adorned and so prettily dressed,
>   in May.
> Sleep, jealous one, and I shall play!

And the Count of Luxembourg began this one for the love of a charming lady who surpassed all others in the performance of songs:

> Down there where flowers grow,
> hold me, lady, hold me in your arms!
> Where rippling waters flow—
>   Ah!
> Hold me in your arms, I know love's sorrow.

And singing in this way they all came back to the comfortable tents freshly strewn with newly cut grasses. The servants had put everything in order, and had removed quilts, beds, and carpets to make more room. They brought water basins since the meal was ready; the tables had been set up and spread with cloths. Then the knights, maidens, and ladies were seated. Conrad, not one to insist on formalities, chose a very modest place (showing extraordinary courtliness). The old Duke of Geneva, wearing fine marten furs around his neck, was given the seat of honor. I'm sure the Bishop of Chartres would rather have been there than at a synod, for this was truly a sight for sore eyes![8] Such bright rosy faces, fine delicate features, arching eyebrows, blond hair, shapely bodies! And when the Count of Sagremor had sung a little song, excellent food was served in brand-new dishes, along with clear cold Moselle wine. There were lots of pastries filled with tender goat meat and plenty of larded venison and good creamy cheese from the Clermont valley. There was plenty of everything you could possibly want for a good summer meal.

Conrad was having a wonderful time, and his gaiety added to everyone's joy. He was the noblest fellow who ever put food or drink in his mouth. He preferred to think of nothing but arms and love; with all his other good qualities, he had not a peer in the world. It made him very happy to see so many maidens and ladies, and so many handsome, worthy knights from his kingdom. When everyone had finished eating, the well-schooled servants were quick to remove the tablecloths. The young men jumped up to get the water basins and pass them around. As you can imagine, there was no lack of volunteers to hold the good king's sleeves, and those of the ladies whose lovely white hands were such a pleasant sight. After everyone who so desired had washed, the shapely ladies slipped on their cloaks, the music started to play, and the fun began.

It wasn't long, I think, before the hunters and archers who had gone out that day, along with those knights who enjoyed such activities, began coming back from different directions, sounding their horns. Their pack-horses were laden with game: young goats, does, and fat stags. When the sound of the horns grew nearer, people were seen carrying the best tidbits on branches and bringing in the carcasses of stags with full racks of antlers. Everyone rushed from the tents to greet those who had taken the lives of so many deer that day. They all said they wished they had gone too.

Those who had beat the bushes returned all shaggy. The hunters were poorly attired in last year's ugly grey traveling cloaks and stiff old red boots. Their hard-paced horses, unable to amble, were bloody to the hocks, and the hunting dogs followed behind them; the men had their leashes tucked under their arms. Without nets or snares they had chased down three stags, and the archers had killed more than twenty does, goats, hares, and foxes who had snatched many a capon from Constant de Noes' farm.[9] The horses were unloaded and the game carried off to be cooked. Since everyone who had gone hunting was dying of hunger, the seneschals had a meal quickly prepared. While the emperor was listening to tall tales, the ladies and maidens went back to the tents, along with those who preferred not to criticize. You might have thought the hunters had been dreaming, so fantastic were their stories. Conrad smiled to himself; that's the way it always is with hunters.

In the late afternoon, a sumptuous supper was prepared. There were many competent and experienced servers trained in court manners, and when it was time to think of setting the table again, there were plenty of young men who knew how to get the job done. They offered water in basins and silver vessels, and then reseated everyone in their former places. The hunters sat all together; they were not as particular about what they ate as were the others, and devoured more than you could possibly imagine. The cooks did the hunters honor by bringing them beef as a first course; it was prepared with good garlic and soaked in grape juice. Then they had young geese and soup mixed with bread and milk. I think that some of the lovers might have enjoyed eating these things, but they were preoccupied with other pleasures. No one, however poor, lacked for food—there was plenty for all. They lacked only the experience of hunger, for the king fed them far too well.

When they had had enough to eat and had drunk their fill of red wine that was far from cheap, the cloths were removed and they all got up from the tables. Then some of them went to play backgammon. Three knights started their dice game again (the maximum stake was six *deniers*), and others sat down to chess or to games of chance. Musicians dressed in ermine wandered among the tents playing their vielles. The ladies and companions of the emperor came out. Young men and graceful maidens removed their cloaks and started to dance hand in hand in the green meadow in front of the tent. A lady dressed in red came forward to sing the first song:

> Away down there in the meadow,
> you do not feel love's sorrow!
> That's where the dancing ladies go;
> watch out for your arms!
> You do not feel love's sorrow
> as I do!

A young fellow belonging to the Provost of Speyer's household sang this song, which was just as pretty:

> Down there under the olive tree
> Robin brings his Marie.
> Water runs bright from the spring,
> under the little olive tree.
> It's true! Robin is bringing
> lovely Marie.

Before he had sung three verses, the clear voice of the Count of Dabo's son, who loved gallant deeds, was heard singing:

> Aelis got up with the sun—
> I'm called Enmelot—
> Adorned and prettily dressed
> beneath Guyon's high crest.
> Lady, on whom shall I bestow
> my love, if I can't have you?

And the Duchess of Austria, renowned for her beauty, began this one:

> The beautiful Aelis gets up with the day.
> Dark and handsome Robin is coming her way.
> She adorns herself and dresses in her best—
> step on the leaves and the flower is for me!
> Coming her way is Robin, love is his quest,
> and even now the meadow smells so sweet.

They sang so much about Robin and Aelis that the dancing lasted till bedtime. If only Lord Eudes de Ronquerolles could have found a king like Conrad![10] But things are different today; you can't find such people. That's why knighthood is on the decline.

They stayed joyfully in the woods for more than two weeks. Before Conrad's guests returned to their lands, the emperor gave them all beautiful gifts. Not one of the ladies or even the least of the maidens left empty-handed. He did them all such great honor that he earned their love and affection. This is the only kind of king who deserves to rule.

Conrad was always convoking assemblies in order to see his knights. He wasn't at all like those kings and great lords who, nowadays, and unfortunately, in my opinion, distribute their sources of revenue and property with abandon to the lowly, thus ruining themselves, their lands, and their people. Such behavior exalts the wicked. It's an evil day when a lord gives a lowborn man a position of power; a peasant will never be anything but a peasant. Our worthy emperor was absolutely opposed to such practices. Positions of authority were reserved for God-loving noblemen who cherished his honor and values as much as their own eyes.

The emperor preferred to let the peasants and townspeople keep what they earned, rather than taking it from them to increase his own wealth. He was wise enough to know it would all be there for him should he need it. Their property and their income were his for the taking; they were only its custodians, even if they were wealthy, well-known merchants. Whenever they attended a fair, they bought fine horses and gifts for the emperor. He gained far more from this than he would have from taxes. He did not allow merchants who traveled through his kingdom, whether or not they were his own subjects, to be bothered for any reason, not even in time of war. He had caused so many thieves to have their eyes put out, and had executed so many highway robbers, that travelers in his kingdom would not have been safer in a church. The noble prince who maintains and rules his lands so wisely is much to be admired.

At that time the Count of Gelderland was at war with the Duke of Bavaria. Neither for love nor for money would the duke agree to a truce. The emperor went to help the count; he reconciled the two of them to such effect that the duke kissed the count, but it was hard work. A valiant lord is well advised to strive for peace.

Conrad was on his way to one of his castles on the Rhine. He went out to ride one morning, when the day had warmed up around nine. After a while he felt bored. He sent a young man to find a minstrel called Jouglet, intelligent, and well known for the great number of wonderful songs and stories he could tell. The young man, the son of a count, finally found Jouglet and brought him to the emperor. Conrad said, "Is it pride or melancholy which makes you avoid my company? A curse on whoever taught you such manners, myself excluded, of course!"[11] He laughed and took hold of Jouglet's bridle, leading him off the path. The emperor said, "I'm sleepy today. How about telling a story to wake me up?" He laughed again and put his left arm around Jouglet's shoulder.

Jouglet said, "This is a true story. Someone who had been in Champagne told me about a marvelous thing that happened there to a worthy and valiant knight. He was handsome and charming, and circumspect in his behavior. He loved a lady who lived in France in the region of Perthois. Nothing on earth could prevent his going to visit her there. Any knight in the world would have felt like a king if he had her love. And as for our young man, Guillaume des Barres in his heyday was nothing compared to him."[12]

Said the emperor, "I'm not sleepy now! I swear I'd see my castle burned to the ground before I get there tonight, and throw in five hundred marks besides, if I could meet such a man. The whole city could burn! God! He could have anything he wanted! With so noble and valiant a friend, that lady was certainly not alone in the world! For Heaven's sake, Jouglet, hurry up and tell me if she was as delightful as he was brave. That would be a miracle."

Said Jouglet, "I've told you about his valor, but that was trivial compared to the beauty of the lady I'm about to describe. Her curly blond hair framed her face, the pink of her cheeks was like roses, the white like lilies, so exquisitely contrasted were the colors. Nature outdid herself—the lady was so beautiful you couldn't find her equal from here to Navarre! Her lovely hazel eyes sparkled like jewels. She had elegantly arched eyebrows, and of course they were not joined together. Her teeth and nose were Nature's finest work." (One who is able to give so charming a description didn't learn his craft yesterday!) "Her face was sweet, her breast and neck white; she was the loveliest lady from here to Dol.[13] She was nobly made; her arms and hands were beautiful. She was so full of courtliness, intelligence, and beauty that even a boor would be transformed by her company. I promise you, she was exactly as I have described her."[14]

"Here, take this fur cloak," said Conrad; "you've certainly earned it. I'd give my right arm to know that such a woman and such a man could still be found in France. I'd forfeit my chance of Paradise, if I didn't send for that knight right away! If he wanted land, a generous lord, and a good friend, he would soon find them in me. As to the lady, what can I say? I know I'll die before finding one like that."

"How can you say such a thing? Right here in your own kingdom lives such a knight, and a lady as beautiful as the one I was telling you about. Everyone who sees her agrees. I can even tell you her name. Her brother is highborn, and worthier than the noble knight in the story."

"My dear Jouglet, if this is true, you were born on a lucky day, and if you can tell me where this handsome, valiant knight has his domain and his home, I swear on my eyes you'll not lack for anything. Has he property? How rich is he?"

Jouglet replied, "Since he was first made a knight, he hasn't been able to maintain six squires, but he and his two companions dress in fur all the time, in summer and winter, because his reputation and fame, his generous heart and his valor provide so well for him that he has land and wealth enough."

"God has certainly given him every good gift. How happy must be the mother of such a noble son! I would be greatly remiss if I didn't make him my knight and companion. Now tell me his name."

"People there call him Guillaume de Dole, though he hasn't any right to the name."

"Then why does he use it?"

"Because he has a house nearby, and Dole sounds more impressive than just the name of the village. Using the name Dole shows good sense rather than guile."

"I think so too," the emperor replied. "What is the name of his sister, who has such a fine and beautiful body?"

"Sire, I will tell you: her name is Liénor."

With this name Love kindled a spark in his breast; from than on all others lost their charm.

"Blessed be the one who gave her that name, and the priest who baptized her! If I were the King of France, he'd be the Archbishop of Rheims."

"Well! All we have to do now is get the two of you together!" said Jouglet.

"Tell me again how beautiful she is."

The minstrel saw perfectly well that just from hearing his words Conrad had fallen in love with Liénor. "Jouglet, tell me everything you can. If she's really half as beautiful as you say, she could be a queen or an empress."

Then Jouglet described the noble maiden in great detail.

"Ah God! She was born lucky—and even luckier is the man she'll love. What we need now is someone to set out early tomorrow morning to find her brother and tell him my heart and my good right arm are at his service."

Jouglet, who was no fool, said merrily, "He won't be that greedy! Your right arm will do for him, believe me! It's the golden-haired Liénor who will have your heart."[15]

"You devil!" said Conrad, with a laugh. "Whatever gives you that idea? What makes you think that I care less about the brother than the sister? She wouldn't be suitable, either for me or for my kingdom; but I'll enjoy thinking about her nevertheless. Meanwhile, we owe her thanks for a pleasant day."

"I'll stop the story here—remind me where I left off.[16] It's time we got back to the road and to our friends."

Conrad replied, "True enough! Let's go." And they sang this song in honor of Gace Brulé:

> When flowers and leaves and grasses fade away,
> the birds no longer have the heart to sing,
> letting the bitter season have its way
> until once more they celebrate the spring.
> But I am singing still, remembering
> my love—God grant me joy of her, I pray—
> for my thoughts are all of her, from her they spring.

Before they had finished, most of the company had arrived at the castle and settled in for the night. The emperor, with a large group of the best knights, was not far behind. They entered the palace through a cypress-wood gate and dismounted. The seneschals were waiting for them; basins of water were brought and tablecloths were spread. Their needs were attended to quickly. After the meal, when everyone had left, Conrad went to get ready for bed. Jouglet was asked to summon a scribe with ink, parchment, and whatever else he required for writing a letter. All three went into the dressing room; Jouglet, who already had Conrad's cloak, stripped him of his tunic as well, while the scribe busied himself writing down what the king dictated. Then the letter was sealed in gold, and a messenger summoned. His name was Nicole. When he arrived, Conrad said, "Take this letter for me to my lord Guillaume de Dole."

I don't know whether Nicole was pleased or not, but he said, "At your service, my lord."

"Let me tell you what's in the letter. He's to get on his horse the moment he's heard it read and, by the faith he owes me, come at once. Even if Guillaume is at a tournament or at war, you're to find him and show my letter; I don't care if your horse drops dead. Just keep your mind on your business."

Nicole was to receive two marks of silver for his expenses, and even more if he thought he would need it. Conrad said he should go right to bed and be off bright and early the next morning. Nicole was even better at carrying messages than an ox at plowing the soil. He got up promptly in the morning, put on his clothes and boots, and got ready for the trip. He mounted his horse and set out, crossing himself as he passed through the town gate. I've never asked where he spent the first night, but I think he was unhappy about traveling alone to Guillaume's house.

Some time after Nicole's departure, the emperor woke up. He asked that a window be opened. His samite coverlet sparkled in the sunlight; it was trimmed with sable and embroidered with golden roses. For love of the fair Liénor, whose name was lodged in his heart, he began this song:

The violets blooming once again in May
and the nightingales a new song demand;
nor would I ever dare to turn away
a new love, the gift of my gentle heart.
May God do me such honor, since her charms
all of my thoughts and all my heart command,
that I'll have held her naked in my arms,
before I leave for the Holy Land.

Thus he comforted himself.

Meanwhile, Nicole, on his long journey to Dole, took care to get up early each morning, so that he could reach his destination in less than a week. Guillaume's widespread fame made him easy to find. Nicole lost no time; at a fast trot, with his head held high, he passed through the village gate, carrying the letter sealed in gold. Such responsibilities weren't new to him, so the first thing he did was take a room and settle in. He had his horse seen to, and changed his boots. His host's daughter brought him a chaplet of flowers and mint. Then he took the letter out of its box and went to Guillaume's house. A boy came running up with a beautiful greyhound, and Nicole learned from him that a meal was about to be served. "I'd better hurry," he said to himself. He straightened his clothes and made sure he looked his best before he went up to the hall.

Guillaume had just come from a big tournament near Rougemont, and the room was crowded with knights and other people. Nicole asked a servant to point out his master before he sat down at the table. Then Nicole went up to Guillaume, removing the cloak from about his neck, so they wouldn't think him a boor. "This letter comes with greetings from the Emperor of Germany. He wants to express his love and esteem for you, and he greatly desires to see you right away."

Guillaume gave him a gracious response. "Brother, may God give the emperor all the joy and honor I wish him. But how is my lord? It's been a long time since I've seen him."[17]

"I left him in good health, praise God."

"I am delighted to hear it."

The knights and everyone else examined the seal. Many of them had never seen one like it. Guillaume sent a servant to Nicole's lodging to make sure he was well taken care of. He took the letter, still unopened, to his mother's room. "Look, my lady, the emperor has sent me a letter sealed in gold. I don't know what's inside, but I'll soon find out."

He pried the seal off with a knife, and took out the letter. He gave the gold seal to his sister, the fair Liénor, to make into a brooch. When she saw the figure of the king mounted and dressed for battle, she exclaimed, "My lady, look! What luck for me that I have a king in my household!"

Guillaume laughed and his mother said, "And so you shall, God and the Holy Spirit willing. I've always known it in my heart."

One of the knights, who was looking over the letter, began to read aloud: "The emperor sends you greetings. He requests that you allow nothing whatsoever to prevent you from coming to him as soon as you have heard this letter. He won't be happy until he sees you."

"You must go, my son," said his mother. "The emperor does you great honor to send for you like this."

"Lady, we'll eat before anything else."

Water was brought for the knights to wash their hands, and then they sat down. Guillaume, who knew what should be done without being told, led the emperor's well-born messenger to a corner of the table where they sat together. There was plenty of meat and fish at the meal. He said, "I'm sure you have often enjoyed better fare. You wouldn't be content with a meal like this in the emperor's household."

"My lord," he replied, "that's perfectly true—we have such an abundance of rotten meat, boar and venison killed out of season, and mouldy old pastries! What the mice reject they give to the squires."

Guillaume spoke to his knights, "I thought we'd stay here at least a week and go hunting, but now I have to leave right away, unless I want to make enemies at court."

"Right!" said Nicole; "that's the truth. Have this table taken away, and let's get everything ready this afternoon so we can leave first thing in the morning."

"Good idea," said Guillaume.

Then they all got up, and Nicole, who wasn't born yesterday, hurried off to make sure that his dappled grey horse had enough to eat. Guillaume went to visit his mother in her rooms. She loved him dearly. When she asked which men he'd be taking with him, he replied, "Lady, for this trip what I need is good company. Two should be enough." He named worthy, well-spoken men, and not too young—both were over thirty. He could be proud of them in the emperor's household.

"Think carefully, my dear," she said. "Be sure you have all you need so that people in Germany won't say you looked needy and poor when you came to court."

The fair Liénor said, "Three new sets of clothes for him are hanging over there. Have the Count of Perche's horse ready and waiting, next to his shield."18

Guillaume, who had won many a battle, sent for his companions. "My lady and I think you two should come with me. Be sure your arms and equipment are in order before the end of the day."

"We have bright new shields, and fine saddles and harnesses for our horses. You won't see three knights so well turned out in a month."

The efficient Nicole had returned to the hall where Guillaume and his two companions came to meet him. Guillaume said, laughing, "I haven't entertained you very well today, but that's your own doing. Everything's ready for us to leave tomorrow morning. Come on," he said, taking his hand, "I'll show you my treasure."

He took him to see his mother and Liénor. Now he has really done something for Nicole; never again will he visit such a beautiful lady in her private rooms. He greeted her, and she him; then he and Guillaume sat down. The golden-haired Liénor, modest and unassuming, sat between them. Her mother, sitting on a large cushion, was embroidering a stole.

"Look at the beautiful work my mother does, Nicole. She is wonderful, and knows everything about sewing. She and my sister embroider all kinds of clerical vestments and decorations for the Church. It's their favorite pastime and also their charity. My mother gives what they make to poor churches in need of ornaments."

"May God grant happiness to me and my children—that's what I pray for every day!"

He said, "Amen to that!"

"Lady," said Guillaume, "it would be nice if you sang us a song."

She loved to sing, and did so willingly. "My dear son," she said, "ladies and queens of days gone by were always singing spinning songs as they embroidered."

"We'd be glad if you'd sing us one now."

"You've asked me so nicely, I can't refuse." Then she began to sing in a pure, clear voice:

> A mother and daughter sit and sew
> crosses embroidered with golden thread.
> Beautiful Aude, she loves Doon so,
> and this is what her noble mother said:
>
> "Learn, my daughter, to weave and to sew
> and embroider crosses with golden thread.
> Get the thought of Doon right out of your head."
> Beautiful Aude, she loves Doon so!

When she had finished, Nicole said, "Your mother sings very beautifully."

"It's true, and now I hope you can hear my sister sing too."

She responded with a smile, knowing that there was no way she could get out of it, once her brother had asked. Her mother said, "You can't refuse to do honor to the emperor's messenger and entertain him."

"I'll be glad to," she replied, and began this song:

> Lovely Aye sits at a cruel lady's feet
> with fine English cloth upon her knee;

the stitches that she makes are small and neat.
Alas! you came from far away,
and now my heart is captured, led astray.

The hot tears keep running down her face,
and cruelly she is beaten early and late
because she loves a knight from a distant place.
Alas! you came from far away,
and now my heart is captured, led astray.

She sang it very sweetly, and then said, "Now, please, that's
enough!"

"Of course, my dear sister, unless, out of the goodness of your heart,
you would let us hear more."

"You know I can't refuse a request from you! But just one more."[19] She
began in a high, clear voice, her golden blond hair shining on her elegant
white tunic:

Lovely Doette, where breezes blow
under the hawthorn, sits waiting for Doon,
grieving and hoping that he will come soon,
wishing her friend were not so slow.
"God! what a noble vassal is Doon!
Dear God, how brave he is! how bold!
I'll love no man, if I can't have Doon."

"How heavy with flowers is the tree
where Doon, my true love, said we would meet!
But he has no wish to come to me . . .
. . . .
God! what a noble vassal is Doon!
Dear God, how brave he is! how bold!
I'll love no man, if I can't have Doon."

When she had finished, she said, "Now you'd be really unkind to ask
again."

The emperor's messenger said, "You're right. And you have the gratitude, love, and thanks of your friends."[20]

They spent the rest of the day together, enjoying themselves until
suppertime. Before the peerless Guillaume went back into the hall, his

mother gave Nicole a purse, and her daughter gave him a brooch from herself and Guillaume, for the love of the emperor. He thanked them profusely and said that he looked forward to returning the favor if he could, that he had never seen such a fine family, and would certainly tell the emperor all about it. He took leave of them with a smile. He and Guillaume went back to the hall where supper was ready. There were lots of different dishes: milk flan, suckling pigs, with which the house was well provided, tasty rabbits, a great abundance of plump larded chickens, and pears and ripe cheeses.

"This is all we can offer you, my friend," said Guillaume, "I'm sorry. You people from the king's household don't know our poor village cooking."

His companions said, "He's pulling your leg."[21]

Nicole replied, "At the emperor's table, I swear you won't dine any better."

So they amused themselves, and enlivened their dinner with talk of chivalry and love. People who conduct themselves this way will make their mark in the world. When the meal was over, the seneschals had the tablecloths removed, and more than twenty servants came with water basins and towels. The squires and lesser folk withdrew. Guillaume chatted with those of his companions who were staying behind; he gave each of them fine gifts, horses, money, as much as they desired. Preparations for the journey had all been made before they went to bed; when the travelers got up in the morning, all they had to do was jump on their horses. You can imagine the many tears they shed when they left. They had three packhorses loaded with clothes and weapons, and fine horses for themselves. Guillaume took affectionate leave of his mother and sister.

"Farewell, dear son!"

"Farewell, dear brother!"

"Farewell, everybody!"

Of course those who stayed behind wept for the two women. There they go! May God be with them!

And so the noble Guillaume de Dole, riding next to Nicole, left the village, which was surrounded by a tall hedge.[22] His mother was sad, of course, and Liénor, too, who was straighter than a sapling and fresher than a rose. Guillaume spent no more than one night anywhere, either to rest or to enjoy himself, so the time passed quickly. On the day he would arrive at court, he and his companions heard the joyful sounds of little birds in the bushes, and they began to sing:

When the days grow long in May,
sweetly a bird sings from afar.
A memory, since I came away,
remains of a love from afar.
And so I wander, bowed with gloom,
where neither song nor hawthorn bloom
are more to me than winter's ice.

When they came to the end of the song, Nicole said joyfully, "We'll soon be there. I should go ahead and arrange lodging for us."

Guillaume replied, "That's a good idea. Take someone with you who can come back and show us the way."

"Come on," he said to a very handsome fellow whose saddle blanket was quilted on both sides. They went galloping off to the castle where the emperor had been staying while Nicole searched for Guillaume. Conrad never rode farther than a league away; instead he had himself bled right there, with only a few congenial people present, instead of the usual crowd.[23] Jouglet was always with him, reminding him of the joy to come. God! The desire in Conrad's heart was driving him insane! That last day he had the sister of a very clever minstrel sing this song by Gerbert[24]:

When Fromont insulted the Hunter,
the good provost had to wait before
a pause came in their clamor;
he leaned on the pommel of his sword.
For Fromont he had no welcome word:
"Fromont," he said, "what I've come here for,
by the will of Gerbert, my noble lord,
who is certainly not a friend of yours,
is to say that he wants to settle a score.
Send Fouques and Rocelin to his court,
for both of them he captured in war.
Should they deny it, he'll restore
their memories with warriors
who will fight for him in any court,
even, with safe conduct, in yours."
Fouques reddened, Rocelin lowered his eyes.
A curse on the one who dares reply!
Old Fromont, enraged, was not so shy.

"Provost, by God, I'll tell you why
your lord in his wisdom chose to confide .
this task to you: you're here to die!
Either he's seen you for the last time,
or he sees you, and you won't be recognized!
I've never gotten out of my mind
the way you once were so very kind
when the French king gave me as a prize
a horse—one hundred pounds was its price—
and you struck it dead; it did not rise.
At Gironville's bridge there was a knight
who gave me such a blow in a fight
that my helmet fell apart and I
grabbed my horse's neck and held on tight."
"Listen to me," Guiret replied,
"it was my son you met in that fight,
and had he not spared you, you would have died.
He'll strike you more blows another time . . ."

Before the song ended, up the stairs came Nicole. He had taken
lodgings for the noble Guillaume, the best available—as Guillaume had
instructed him—on an upper floor with lots of windows. They had strewn
the floors and decorated the windows with greenery. The others had
followed so quickly behind him that they were soon at the inn where their
arrival caused great excitement.

Even as Guillaume and his two companions were dismounting, Nicole
appeared before Conrad, who said, "Well?"

"Good news!"

"Did you find my lord Guillaume?"

"I certainly did, and there's not his equal in all of France!"

"Wonderful! Will he dine with us?"

"I really don't know! I've already found him lodgings in town."

Jouglet jumped up and said, "By God! I'll go get him!"

"Aha, Jouglet! Now we shall see just how well you can convey my
greetings! Tell him he has come to the right place, and that I want to see
him."

Jouglet set out immediately.

The emperor drew Nicole away from the others toward the chapel:
"Tell me the truth! Did you see his sister?"

"Hush! Say no more! No one should talk of such a miracle unless he's just been to confession. She has no equal for beauty and modesty. Everyone who hears her sing says her voice is the sweetest of melodies, and they are right."

"How do you know?"

"I heard her."

Conrad was all ears. "Come on! Is she really so beautiful?"

"Absolutely! And not just part of her but all of her—arms, body, head, and face. The fair Liénor's beauty surpasses all others just as gold surpasses all other metals."

"She is worthy of her name then,"[25] said the emperor. "And what can you tell me about her brother? I'm looking forward to meeting him."

"Well, he's a very handsome knight; his chest is broad, his arm is strong, he has curly auburn hair, his face is slender with fine features. He has bold laughing eyes and good broad shoulders."[26]

"If he really looks like that, he's a lucky man, the sort of knight they tell about in fairy tales!"

"That's just what you'll say when you see him. He lives extremely well. If a great lord kept such a household, his vassals would be a force to be reckoned with. As it is, Guillaume has so many knights and other people around him that you can hardly move."

"Go to his inn right away and be sure that he has everything he wishes. I can't wait till he gets here."

Nicole left, and the king, in a very good mood, stayed behind waiting to entertain Guillaume de Dole, whom Jouglet had gone to fetch from his inn. If the knight's sister could only be with him, Conrad's joy would be complete. The king was so strangely elated he couldn't keep still. Overjoyed at Guillaume's arrival, he suddenly began to sing the song by Renaut de Beaujeu, the good knight from Rheims:

> When true love dwells within a heart that's pure,
> never can it be banished or let go;
> whatever torments lovers must endure
> seem a happiness and bring no sorrow.
> Who understands true love will seek no cure,
> but welcome grief and torment as a treasure.
> All this must every lover come to know.
>
> If someone says that death is all his prize
> for loving faithfully, that is not true.

A lover is false who profits from disguise—
may God give every counterfeit his due!
Lovers may die of love, but if they do,
on Judgment Day to glory they'll arise;
so love makes me hold most dear what I most rue.

Nothing, believe me, was bothering Conrad. Jouglet had gone to look for the noble knight. When he reached the top of the stairs, before he had even entered the room, he shouted, "Dole! Valiant knight! Guillaume! Where is the rising star, the pride and joy of the kingdom?"

Guillaume jumped up, "What? Ah, Jouglet! Where did you come from, dear friend?" He threw his arms around his neck, overjoyed to see him.

Jouglet said, "I'm so glad you are here! And our good emperor sends his warmest greetings. In fact, he can't wait to see you."

They went over to a window and sat down. Jouglet told Guillaume everything he had done and how it was all arranged, how the king had had the letter written and sent to him because of Jouglet's story. "What more can I tell you! You are the most powerful man at court right now." He threw his arms joyfully around Guillaume's neck. "Dear friend, let me embrace you! This is your lucky day! We've been waiting a long time to welcome you here."

"You have my thanks. I'm very glad to know all this, and the real reason why the king sent for me."

"Be happy then."

Nicole had come back and ordered dinner: meats and whatever else was available, good wines and cream-filled pastries. When the food was ready, servants brought it upstairs. Guillaume asked them to send for the host and his wife. And Jouglet said, "Tell the lady to bring along her lovely daughter. She's the best-dressed girl in town."

The servants spread cloths on the green grass and over fine cushions. The knights washed their hands and then sat down to a light meal; now they wouldn't get too hungry before dinner that night. Jouglet said, "I'm afraid the emperor will be annoyed by this delay."

As soon as he had eaten, Guillaume put on a cloak of fine silk, dark as blackberries, lined in delicately scented fine ermine.

"Good lord!" said Jouglet, "Now I see what French clothes look like!"

The handsome and noble Guillaume was so generous that his companions also wore cloaks lined with sweet-smelling black sable and miniver.

Eudes de Rades de Crouci, for all his wealth, never looked as elegant as these three.[27] The girl gave each of them a chaplet of lovely blue flowers. The chamberlain brought them white gloves and new belts. While they were getting dressed, their horses were brought around, beautiful big warhorses from Spain, with finely-worked leather gear from Limoges. When they came down from their rooms, the hostess made very sure that Guillaume saw her shapely young daughter. Mounted on his horse, he really looked like a great lord.

"Brother Jouglet," said Guillaume, "Why don't you jump up behind me."

The girl said, "Jouglet, I'm furious with you! You haven't sung once since you came through our door."

Guillaume laughed at that and said, "She's right!"

"You'll have to forgive me," Jouglet said.

"I'll be glad to, if you'll come back tonight with your vielle."

"Indeed I will, if we can have some dancing."

And so she kept them there with her charming conversation. Of course they were delighted with their chaplets. My lord Guillaume draped his cloak over his left arm. Every one from the inn and all the neighbors admired him no end, while Jouglet sang in his ear:

> Aelis arose very early—
> Greetings to her with all my heart!
> Dressed and adorned to look her best
> under the alder tree.
> Greetings to her with all my heart!
> It's not with me.

Off they went, down the street. Not a person within a stone's throw failed to come and look at them.

"May God grant you good fortune," said the townspeople.

"These are not people to be trifled with!" they murmured to each other.

Guillaume and Jouglet went their way without stopping, their horses at the walk. There were plenty of people to hold their stirrups for them when they arrived. When the king and his household saw the knight from their window, Conrad said, "By all the saints! He's just what they said he'd be!" And turning to the Count of Forez, he asked, "When did you last see a knight like this one? And you won't see one again between now and the Saint Denis fair."[28]

In short, no knight has been so joyously welcomed at an emperor's court since the days of the Trojan Paris![29] Long live the man who deserves such honor!

"Dear friend," said the Emperor Conrad, "I can't tell you how happy I am to see you here at last. I've been longing to meet you. In fact, I've stayed here waiting for you these last two weeks."

True love has great ennobling power. Hand in hand they went to the table, and the others, two by two, followed them. The emperor wanted Guillaume to sit next to him, but the young man wouldn't allow it. He had only just arrived, and was careful not to appear lacking in courtesy. He and his companions sat a little below the emperor.

Conrad asked Guillaume if he knew the King of England, with whom our French kings had long been at war.[30] At this first meeting with Conrad, Guillaume distinguished himself by his excellent manners. His companions also knew how to conduct themselves, and talked of various things with the emperor's companions. Ah! Had it been proper to do so, Conrad would have spoken of quite another subject! Not how to put roofs on churches or how to make roads, but of the noble, lovely maiden who had set his heart on fire.

At that point Jouglet, who knew how to move an ox,[31] whispered to Guillaume, "Don't give him your pedigree; talk about jousting and love. Two weeks from Monday there'll be a tournament at Saint-Trond."[32]

"That's wonderful, Jouglet! Let's all go!" replied Guillaume straight away. "All I need is a helmet—I have everything else: leggings, hauberks, and my horse who's as brave as a lion, strong and agile and fast."

Said Jouglet, "I promise we'll find you a helmet."

"I lost mine the other day when I was captured at Rougemont."

The king, in his generosity, said: "You shall have the best and most elegant helmet in all Germany. It was made in Senlis. I guarantee you could build a great tower for the price of its jewels and gold."

Conrad ordered Boidin the Fleming, his chamberlain, to bring the helmet, which had been acquired some time ago, along with a hauberk from Chambly. The chamberlain knew where it was and brought it quickly. He took it out of its case and polished it with a towel. "What a beauty!" exclaimed Guillaume. "You wouldn't find its equal in two kingdoms!"[33] This was no ordinary gift—an emperor so generous with his treasures will have no lack of noble knights. Then Conrad picked it up by the noseguard and handed it to him.

"It's yours," he said, "and it won't be your only gift from me."

"Sire," said Guillaume, "may God reward you."

Everyone who looked at the helmet saw himself reflected as in a mirror. "Now he has no excuse for not going to the tournament," said Guillaume's companions.

"Right you are!" said the emperor. "And then we'll see who will carry off the prize."

When they had finished looking at the helmet, the chamberlain put it back in its case. Guillaume said, "Put it away for now. You'll accompany me to my lodgings tonight and bring it with you."

Guillaume and his two companions were surrounded by people eager to get to know them. The servants sent to ask the cook if they could put the tablecloths on. That was all there was left to do before the meal was ready. Without waiting a moment longer, the king washed his hands and went to sit down at the table, with six dukes and counts in attendance, and he seated his new guest close to him with just one count between them. I won't bother to tell you about the others since they belonged to the king's household. Nor will I describe the food and the presents, except to say that everyone had whatever his heart desired, without having to wait or make a fuss. There was much talk of the tournament during the meal, and, as always happens, many spoke who were better at words than at fighting (not a great quality in a gentleman). But Guillaume let them talk on and said nothing. The emperor, watching him with affection, saw that he was keeping his thoughts to himself. In fact, Guillaume was thinking that, in honor of his new helmet, he would defeat everyone at the tournament, fair return for the gift!

They left the table and the emperor washed his hands. The young squires and uncongenial people left the palace, which was so large you could gallop a horse inside. Then the minstrels arrived and strolled among the noble lords, each playing a different instrument. One told of Perceval, another of Roncevaux. Our Guillaume had had enough experience of the world to know how to engage in polite conversation. After a while, the emperor silently took his hand and led him away. They sat down on a bed, and rather than hear more about Charlemagne, Conrad spent the evening asking Guillaume about himself. He didn't dare to speak of what was dearest to his heart because someone might overhear. Jouglet entertained them with songs and told three or four bawdy tales.[34] The emperor sang this song for Guillaume's pleasure:

> It's been so long
> since I last heard
> the turtledove's summer song

in the old sweet way;
but love leads me astray,
bewilders me,
keeps all my thoughts on her,
wherever I may be.

They sat on the silk coverlet enjoying themselves until it was time for bed. The king said, "I'll be going, but after all that singing, let's have a drink first." They called for wine stewards, and right away a chamberlain appeared; the goblet in his hand looked like a jewel set in gold. Liénor's brother drank first after the king. I don't know who was last, but when everyone had been served, Guillaume asked a servant to call Boidin, who had brought him his helmet. Hand in hand Guillaume and the emperor went out to find Guillaume's horses, which were ready at the steps.

"You're dead if you don't sleep late tomorrow morning!" said the king. They were tired from their travels, so these were welcome words. Jouglet was persuaded to bring his vielle back to their lodgings, as they had promised the young lady. They mounted two on each horse, Boidin with my lord Guillaume, Jouglet with one of Guillaume's companions.

When they arrived at the inn, people hastened to light many torches. The lovely Aelis was there. They dismounted and went to the upper floor, where servants brought plenty of good fruit and wine. The hostess and her daughter joined them and they all stayed, singing and laughing and having a wonderful time, until close to midnight. When Boidin said he must leave, the noble Guillaume had one of his servants bring out a magnificent sleeveless tunic lined with whole squirrel furs; it had been made that very week and was still fragrant from the dye. The chamberlain accepted the splendid gift with thanks. "Ah!" Jouglet exclaimed, "How perfect for summer!"

Guillaume gave the innkeeper a traveling cloak which was also new and perfumed with the scent of dye. And without an instant's delay he handed Jouglet his own cloak made of ermine. There was nothing else to do, if he wanted to part with all he had.

Guillaume presented a fine brooch to the innkeeper's wife, saying, "Take good care of it, dear hostess, it's quite priceless! If you wear it at your throat, you can drink all the wine in Orleans and never get drunk!"

"If only it were mine," exclaimed the host. "I drink my fill every day!"

Guillaume gave the young lady his silver-trimmed belt to reward her for singing this new song to Jouglet's accompaniment:

> Perronele was in the meadow;
> now I'm happy in love again!
> Washing her clothes in the brook—
> now I'm happy in love again!
> One look
> that's all it took.

Boidin said, "Jouglet certainly told us the truth, my lord, about your ways."

And the host added, "He has been more than kind to us ever since he arrived. I'm sure he'll be richly rewarded some day for that squirrel-lined cloak and those sables dark as mulberries."

Boidin didn't stay any longer. He went down the stairs, in great good humor, mounted, and rode back to court. Wearing his new tunic he went straight to the emperor, to sing Guillaume's praises. Conrad had just retired for the night. As soon as he saw Boidin he said, "Who gave you that tunic?"

"No usurer, you can be sure! You've never met anyone so noble and generous. In the short time I was visiting him, he gave away furs and jewels worth at least a hundred pounds."

"He'd better watch out or he'll soon be out of money," the emperor said.

"Don't worry, Sire. The townspeople will be glad to lend him more— he gives them presents and treats them respectfully. Besides which he pays on time."

"He's certainly made good use of that tunic; it is said that to give is to be a king."

Then they hurried off to bed. Thanks to the talk and his drowsiness the emperor went to sleep right away. In the morning he had a kind and noble thought: he sent Guillaume five hundred pounds worth of Cologne money, knowing that he would need it to accomplish his desires. And before Guillaume's companions were out of their beds they received two excellent war horses and two large silver goblets. They thanked the emperor when they went to mass. Unexpected gifts are best, and reflect great honor on the giver.

"You've certainly done your good deed for the day," said Guillaume to the king who replied,

"That's the way God takes care of those in my service. You must be often in need of money, or so says Boidin." Just then arrived Jouglet draped in his ermine cloak.

"My dear friend!" the emperor exclaimed, "Some madman must have stripped himself naked for you!"

Jouglet replied, "And right he was! He looks fine in his fur-lined green, and this cloak is just what I needed."

No little time was spent during the church service discussing Guillaume's costly gift.

Right after breakfast, Guillaume dictated three letters to a scribe. The first was for his mother, telling her how high he was in the emperor's good graces. He sent a belt and brooch to his sister, and with it a metal box containing three hundred pounds from what Conrad had given him. That would pay his creditors and the servants. His mother, needless to say, would also make good use of the money, to have her flax sown and for household expenses. Only those who have had similar responsibilities can appreciate what is involved.

Guillaume also wrote to his friends, telling them how things were with him and asking each one of them, God willing, to meet him without fail at Saint-Trond. They were to equip themselves as elegantly as they could; he was looking forward to jousting with beautifully painted lances. Another letter was sent in all haste to Liège, where there was a friendly supplier who would let him order on credit. Guillaume asked for one hundred and twenty lances painted with his arms, and three shields with fittings of silk and brocade. Each one of the lances, he particularly insisted, was to have a pennant. Everything was done as he had requested, and even better.

You should have seen the preparations for the tournament! In two weeks everything was ready—shields and lances, coverings for the horses, banners of taffeta and silk. Meanwhile the emperor, tired of staying in one place, made the time pass more quickly by moving to Maastricht on the Moselle. The setting was very beautiful, and they spent the very shirts off their backs on the wonderful wines of the region. They dined on every kind of game you could imagine, and birds and fish from the river. It was a truly enjoyable place, and only eight leagues away from the tournament. Conrad made it no secret that he intended to see for himself who the champion would be. I know he carried out his plan, but I'm not sure how long the journey to Maastricht took. In any case, the townsfolk were more than happy to welcome him on his arrival. Conrad was born under a lucky star: to see him was to love him.

My lord Guillaume and many others from court, counts and barons included, sent their servants to Saint-Trond to find suitable lodgings. None were more capable than Guillaume's, and he made them swear on their eyes that he would have the best rooms, no matter what the cost. And he did well to insist, because they found exactly what he needed: a manor house whose courtyard barns and stables could easily accommodate fifty knights and all their equipment without the slightest crowding or discomfort. Guillaume, saving God's displeasure, would be arriving with a very large company. Meanwhile he stayed in Maastricht, living in a palace on the river. The emperor was very kind to him, and showed his affection with beautiful gifts.

Conrad often thought of his beloved. One day when he was standing with Guillaume in the alcove of a window, he suddenly saw Jouglet and asked him to sing this song:

> In this bitter time of the year
> when frost makes the branches white,
> I choose to sing, despite
> my sadness, for all to hear.
> This is my grievance and my plight:
> because I would never cheat,
> Love has brought me to defeat,
> because I would never lie,
> Love's favor has passed me by.

Our Guillaume had no such reason to be sad; that evening he had his doublet covered with gold-embroidered silk. He concealed as best he could his elaborate plans for the tournament. The emperor, so well-disposed toward Guillaume, would not find out a thing unless he guessed. He would see the results soon enough; there was no need for Guillaume to boast.

Guillaume took his leave the day before the tournament was to begin. The emperor was sorry to let him go, so much did he enjoy his company. Guillaume had persuaded thirty of Conrad's knights, armed and mounted, to come with him. A nobleman's life is hard! His equipment got to Saint-Trond before he did. As soon as he arrived they showed him the shields, saddle blankets, lances, and banners. "God's blessing on my good friend in Liège!" he exclaimed.

That worthy and noble gentleman had traveled with the equipment. Right out in the open he said that Guillaume was welcome to everything he had. His words showed his wisdom; a man won't lose by being courteous when it is appropriate.[35] Knights from far and near filled the inns in the town. Guillaume's was well-situated at a crossroads; from the upstairs windows you could see in both directions. The balcony overlooked the marketplace, where if you didn't look sharp you got your toes stepped on, as many a rustic fellow discovered to his pain.[36]

One Sunday morning Guillaume's companions arrived from Dole. He embraced them all and asked how things were. "Wonderful!" they said, "All's well at home."

"What's the word? Are lots of people coming?"

"Hundreds and thousands! There won't be a good knight left in Perche, Poitou or Maine, and the Count of Champagne is bringing as many as he can persuade to come."

"Do you think the French and Flemish knights will be there?"

"Well, we know (or at least we've heard) that the lords of Ronquerolles, Barres, and Coucy are coming, along with Alain de Roucy, Gaucher de Châtillon, and someone from Maulion. We're sure about these—they spent last night at Namur."

"And you who were at Ligny, what do you know about Gaucher de Joigny—the one who almost died for love of his lady? Have you heard whether he's coming?"

"Yes! God brought him back to life—he's all ready to joust."

"I'm certainly happy to hear it."

"Don't worry—lots of people are on their way. Count Renaut de Boulogne spent last night at Mons in Hainaut."

Guillaume threw his hands in the air for joy. His companions said: "And if there aren't enough fighters on your side, you'll be surrounded by so many servants you'll scarcely be able to break a lance."[37]

"We're pretty sure of the good knight from Saxony and of the duke, if nothing prevents him from coming. And the Count of Dabo will be with us too, and the black-haired Galeran de Limbourg and his father the duke and five or six counts."

"And what about the noble Count of Bar, whose father had no equal for valor and courage?"

"He's coming, splendidly equipped, with a great number of men from Lorraine, great jousters all of them, and every baron from here to the Rhine. You'll see any number of great lords from Hainaut and Burgundy arrive this morning with wonderful fighting gear. They'll be in the castle here and nearby. You can see their shields already, hanging on gables all around the square."

Since there will be no end of coming and going for quite some time, let's discuss the dinner. Enough about fighting! I'd rather talk about food.

Everyone had exactly what he wanted, there was no need even to ask. Guillaume did his best to honor those who came with him from court, embracing this one, running to welcome that one, turning to greet another, and then another. If someone was higher in rank, Guillaume took care to receive him accordingly; he was skilled at giving his guests the deference they were due. No wonder the emperor thought so well of him!

Before they had finished their meal, so many groups of horsemen had arrived from every direction, it seemed three such towns couldn't have accommodated a quarter of them. You never saw anyone as busy as those knights, finding lodgings for themselves and settling in, hanging their pennants and banners from the rain gutters to show their friends where they were. All those people yelling in Flemish, "Boidin! Boidin!" or "Wautre! Wautre!" made you think the town was full of devils. They shouted and fooled around all night long. Half of them still hadn't found lodgings when Jouglet, who had spent the morning at Maastricht sleeping like a log,[38] came riding a Norwegian palfrey in search of Guillaume. No need for him to ask where Guillaume was staying! It was easy to pick out the best inn, the one with the greatest number of knights and servants. Indoors were countless heralds and minstrels making a racket. I don't know whether it was God or the devil who had told them, perhaps in a dream, where to find the generous knight. Possessions come from God, and Guillaume was always eager to give them away; a worthy man is satisfied with little.[39]

Jouglet went up the stairs and found both lodgings to his liking and his favorite young knight. Guillaume was wearing a splendid shirt, and over it only a sleeveless tunic with a band of English brocade across the back. You'd have to look far and wide to find its equal: it was lined with scarlet silk, and its collar was fine ermine. On his head was a lovely chaplet of pearls[40] and gold buttons.

"Well! If it isn't Jouglet! A great companion *you* turned out to be! If only we'd traveled together, you'd now be the proud owner of that tunic over there!" (But Jouglet knew he'd get it anyway.) "Who were you with?"

"A lot of Germans—I nearly died of boredom! And I'm starved—I've had nothing to eat all day long. Hey! Someone bring me a drink!"

"What the devil, Jouglet! Go on back to your Germans!"

Guillaume ordered a pie with two gelded peacocks in it to be brought right away.[41] It was almost time for vespers and they would have to hurry. Some of the knights had sworn not to bear arms on Sunday, and Guillaume was one of them. "Mount up! Let's go!" said Jouglet, striking his bow against the vielle. Then saddles were flung on the horses—black, chestnut,

and piebald—which were led out by the hundreds onto the street. A young rider from Normandy began to sing this song, with Jouglet accompanying him:

> In a royal chamber, beautiful Eglantine
> was sewing a shirt, with her mother there to see,
> . . . . .⁴²
> when thoughts of love enflamed her suddenly.
>   Now hear the tale—
>   Eglantine's wit did not fail.

> She cuts and sews the cloth; the lady stays.
> Eglantine had more skill on other days.
> She pricks her finger when her attention strays—
> all this her mother notices right away.
>   Now hear the tale—
>   Eglantine's wit did not fail.

> "Eglantine," said her mother, "please undress.
> . . . .
> I want to see your body's loveliness."
> "No, my lady, it's cold; I'll catch my death."
>   Now hear the tale—
>   Eglantine's wit did not fail.

> "Beautiful Eglantine, what is the matter?
> It seems to me you're pale and getting fatter."
> . . . .
> . . . .
>   Now hear the tale—
>   Eglantine's wit did not fail.

> "From you, my gentle lady, I can't hide
> the truth: I fell in love with a valiant knight;
> that is Henri, in whom his lord takes pride.
> So may your love take pity on my plight."
>   Now hear the tale—
>   Eglantine's wit did not fail.

> "Eglantine, will the noble Henri marry you?"
> "I don't know, mother, I never asked him to."
> . . . .
> . . . .

Now hear the tale—
Eglantine's wit did not fail.

"My lovely Eglantine, go right away
and tell Henri from me that he must say
whether he'll be your husband or leave you this way."
And Eglantine replied, "I will obey."
Now hear the tale—
Eglantine's wit did not fail.

From her mother's house fair Eglantine sped;
to Henri's lodging her footsteps led.
She found her lover lying in bed,
and you shall hear what words she said.
Now hear the tale—
Eglantine's wit did not fail.

"Are you awake or sleeping, my lord knight?
Eglantine, whose eyes like stars are bright,
asks if you'll have her for your wedded wife."
"Yes!" said Henri, "I've not known such joy in my life."
Now hear the tale—
Eglantine's wit did not fail.

Henri has listened to her with great delight.
He quickly summons twenty of his knights
and to his country joyfully they ride;
now she is his countess and his bride.
How happy Count Henri is
that the beautiful Eglantine is his!

To the sound of flutes and vielles, Guillaume, accompanied by all kinds of princes and counts, went to watch the jousting. (This was no ecclesiastical debate!) Guillaume rode behind his banners, with sixty companions of great valor and fame, to see if anyone was on the field. Vivien at Aliscans did no such valiant deeds as Guillaume was planning to do the next day, may God help him![43] Seeing him there, radiant in his fine sleeveless tunic, his eyes bright and shining, many a noble maiden wished him good luck.

As they rode through the gates of the town, they had a different kind of greeting from a knight much in favor with the Duke of Louvain. He came galloping up in perfect control of his horse, and said that no one was to go out to the field.

"Please tell us what's happening, my noble lord," they said.

"The feast of Saint George the Martyr⁴⁴ is to be celebrated at the castle tonight."

They stopped in a big barley field to talk about it. "We might as well go back," they all agreed, and so they did. Their splendid attire had not suffered in the least. They spent the rest of the day exploring their lodgings, enjoying the food and game of the season, and also the fine dry wines. When the lamps were lit in the evening, anyone looking at the town from a distance would have thought Guillaume's inn was on fire. The light shining out of its windows reached beyond the market place, and all the streets around it were bright as day. How could a young knight be more splendidly lodged? The sound of vielles and flutes and other instruments would have drowned out God's thunder.

Although many of the knights wandered about from place to place, Guillaume stayed where he was, waiting for the others to visit him. And this was a good idea, because then they could see how many valiant warriors were there, and how lively and joyful everyone was. All the dukes and other noblemen lodged in the nearby inns were drinking merrily at Guillaume's—not talking of weapons but rather dancing so boisterously they could be heard throughout the town. The handsome Galeran de Limbourg, who hadn't been so cheerful for ages, began this song:

> Where the olive tree bends low,
> don't be sorry for what you do.
> Clear and bright runs the spring—
> dance, maidens! dance in a ring!
> Don't be sorry for what you do
> when your love is true.

Three times around and the Count of Maastricht's son, who sang very well, began this one:

> Mauberjon got up early today
> and dressed in her best,
> out for joy, hooray!
> To the spring she made her way,
> I'm sorry to say.
> Oh, God! God! Too long
> By the water does Mauberjon stay.

And then a young man from the Count of Looz's court, another fine singer, began:

> Across a field Renaut rides with his lady,
> they ride through the dark until the sun shines bright.
> My love of you is lost to all delight . . .

So the young men amused themselves. Even the most lavish spender could not have failed to be pleased. The Count of Bar stayed a long time, and one of the emperor's minstrels sang for him this song about his brother:

> Of Renaut de Mousson
> and Hugh his brother,
> and his companions,
> generous to others,
> there'll be a new song—
> old Jordain will make one—
> ere the harvest is done.

They talked a long time about Jordain. "Are we going to keep this up all night?" said a Fleming.

"We'll see!" they replied. "The first to leave will be first in courtesy."[45] At that the noisy festivities came to an end. No one who attended will ever hear of a better party anywhere. But it was time for them to find their beds, many of which were furnished with fine sheets and coverlets. Competent servants arranged everything quickly and quietly, and then helped their masters to bed. There wasn't much of the night left!

The morning was fine and clear, like summertime. And when the knights awoke Guillaume had their shields and lances with beautiful pennants displayed at all the windows, so that the town looked three times as splendid as before.

When it was time to go to church, he was accompanied not by three but by some sixty knights, all elegantly attired and mounted on fine horses. They rode two by two in front of him and beside him. The innkeeper's son, always eager to serve Guillaume, followed close behind him to give the offering. They heard a mass in honor of the Holy Spirit, beautifully sung and recited by one of the abbess's chaplains, and then they returned to the inn. The wine stewards and cooks were asked to bring a suitable pre-tournament meal, but they hadn't been long at table when five or six groups of warriors started out. They had been hearing noise from the melee for quite some time.

My lord Guillaume's companions and his household occupied a good part of the marketplace, since one hundred and forty servants were required just to carry his lances; every one of them wore a chaplet. There were plenty of other people too, and minstrels making a lot of noise with their various instruments. Everyone shouted, "May God grant him success!"

Those who were handing out one by one the innumerable lances also gave each knight a pair of white gloves and a new belt. This gracious gesture from Guillaume was much noticed and talked about. Splendidly attired, the knights rode in pairs, side by side, their painted lances upright, the banners waving behind them. Then came three matched warhorses, each one draped in gold brocade beautifully embroidered with coats-of-arms that cost, believe it or not, at least one hundred Cologne *sous*. Next came three beautiful shields, and never had any been so ceremoniously treated. They were carried by three of the emperor's noblemen. These were wearing elaborate tunics without cloaks, and held the shields high against their chests like treasures or holy relics.

Thus, in great splendor, my lord Guillaume left his lodgings. His was the finest horse in the tournament. It was whiter than new-fallen snow, and draped all the way to the ground in bright red openwork samite which made a beautiful contrast with the white. When someone tries so hard to distinguish himself, it's no wonder if he succeeds!

Under his hauberk he wore only a padded doublet; a simple chaplet of flowers adorned his head. As he mounted, he asked God to preserve him from shame. Slowly he rode away through the joyful tumult, his companions following two by two just like a procession of monks. And Jouglet, with Aigret de Grame, was singing this song:

> Under the branches bending low,
> that's the way true lovers should go,
> bright are the flowing waters there.
> Oh!
> So let him love whose lady's fair.

Before the end of it, two young men, nephews of lord Dinant, began another which suited them very well:

> To the shore of the sea,
> now lightly you must go!
> That's where the dance will be.
>   I'll be there too.
> Now lightly you must go,
>   two by two!

A great many congenial people had gone upstairs to watch from windows and balconies. Highborn ladies of the region stood at the windows and doors; not one who was young and beautiful had stayed at home. Even the maidens from Done had come in carriages. Flowers (and not mere violets) adorned countless chaplets. "God!" said one of the ladies, "who's the man in the wonderful tunic?"[46]

"That's the valiant Guillaume de Dole—isn't he good looking!"

"Anyone he loves would certainly love him back! The one who wins his heart is a lucky lady!"

Everyone who saw Guillaume agreed: "He's even better looking than Graelent Muer!"[47] With their hearts and their eyes they followed him down the street.

Now something extraordinary happened, by which God increased Guillaume's renown.[48] The emperor, spurring his horse, arrived in the midst of all this merriment. He heard the sound of flutes and vielles, and saw how the ladies and maidens were gazing at Guillaume. "Few men are as charming as he," Conrad thought. And forcing his way through the crowd, he threw his arms around Guillaume's neck. "Guillaume! By Saint Paul, where have you been hiding!"

Nothing could have been a greater honor. Guillaume rode in glory next to the emperor out into the countryside where, in all their finery, Conrad's people and the high lords of the Empire, with countless spirited horses and untold numbers of colorful flags and banners, spread over a vast field.

Near a hill, where the wheat stood tall and green, Guillaume dismounted with his friends and his company. Each of them stuck his lance in the ground; the row they formed was so long you couldn't shoot an arrow half as far. In sixty or even a hundred places you would have seen servants unloading packhorses, emptying bright new carrying cases over traveling cloaks spread on the ground, pulling out hauberks and elegant white leggings. Some brought needles and thread for sewing up sleeves, others put on epaulettes. Meanwhile their masters went about greeting people—

cries of "Wilecome!" and "Godehere!" resounded from all sides, and hundreds of voices were heard demanding girths, surcingles, helmet lacings. I can tell you that those who dressed Guillaume in his armor were masters of their craft; needless to say he looked wonderful.

When his helmet was laced up, he attached to the top of it a pennant showing the king's arms. The Count of Clèves, in a great rush to be first, was already on his way with a hundred knights all galloping together. The emperor and the Count of Alost went to watch the French warriors who were advancing in tight ranks. Unless some fault of theirs, or God's will, prevents it, by nightfall they will all be exhausted from fighting, since they truly hope to distinguish themselves on this promising occasion.

Guillaume's companions had mounted, and he himself was in the saddle, his warhorse entirely draped in fine fabric. He wasn't exactly the picture of gloom, nor was his handsome face covered with blemishes. He said, "Let's go and see what they're up to; we can leave most of the lances and gear for now." So he had them take just thirty lances and hung his bright new shield around his neck by its fine strap of gold brocade. Pricking his horse with his spurs, he quickly set out toward the fighting. Sixty companions, fully armed, accompanied him, their helmets laced up and banners unfurled in the wind; some hundred heralds followed, calling attention to his presence. Everyone said "Let him through! It's Guillaume de Dole! Hurrah!"

To the sound of flutes and reed pipes they escorted him to the front line. He looked about and saw a Fleming who had picked up his shield to joust. God! What a lot of noble lords were watching! There he was out in front with his large company.[49] He had moved his elbow against his shield so that the strap snapped into his fist; as soon as he saw his opponent he went for him at a gallop—and took, believe me, a heavy blow. Neither hauberk nor the doublet underneath were damaged, but a full measure of iron and wood from the lance went through his shield. It was only thanks to God that he wasn't wounded. But our Guillaume responded with a blow that didn't come from a beginner. Striking high against the middle of the chest, his heavy lance knocked his opponent right off his horse. Said Jouglet: "Dole! Knights! It's Guillaume the Spear Collector!"[50] Guillaume's companions dashed up like a flock of starlings, and soon the man had no choice but to give up and admit defeat. Guillaume took the horse for his man from Liège.[51]

Men from Valécourt and Artois charged together, and Guillaume, spurring his horse, advanced to meet them. But before he could use his lance, some seven or eight of them attacked, striking Guillaume on his helmet and on his shield; nevertheless, he returned a masterful blow. He struck his opponent's helmet above the noseguard, and, with the full length of the lance, sent him crashing to the ground. But many harsh blows he took before he would even talk of surrendering! Guillaume, who had no intention of letting him off, sent him as a prisoner to his host at Saint-Trond. Jouglet got the horse.

Guillaume's companions weren't easy to deal with either! They slashed, cut, and split so many shields and helmets that five men from Artois were captured during the battle. The knights from Alost, Walincourt, and Bailleul stayed so close together that no one could break through their ranks.

Guillaume had fought eight jousts in rapid succession, and his lord the emperor had seen them all. He had won seven of them, and taken seven horses. He was careful to remain well in sight on the outer ranks. Glory was what he sought, and his shield showed it—there were so many holes and tears that, even counting the strap, I don't think a full hand's breadth was left.

While someone was handing him another one, he saw the worthy Michel de Harnes[52] coming toward him, his lance at rest, holding his shield by the armstrap, and looking for action. Guillaume grabbed his shield and a new lance and sped off faster than a swallow, holding his shield at an angle in front of him. Michel didn't hesitate; he came galloping up on a sleek roan to strike Guillaume a fair blow in the upper center of his shield—a dangerous spot, under the collarbone, only a few inches from his neck. He might have unhorsed Guillaume, had his lance not snapped in two. Guillaume struck back; holding steady a heavy lance, stiff as a club, he hit Michel twice in the center of his shield, over his chest. Horse and rider had charged with such abandon that Michel's girths and chest harness snapped like old leather lacing, and he, still seated in the saddle, flew over the horse's tail. Guillaume's extraordinary feat required great strength. He whirled around, grabbed Vairon's reins, and presented the horse to one of the emperor's men who had been captured.

"He certainly knows how to win friends and fame," said the emperor to a nobleman standing near him.

"Right! Even Roland would be no match for him! This man is the pearl of warriors, the best in the whole tournament. You see how everyone gets out of his way—no one can face him and survive."

Once vanquished and taken prisoner, Michel was allowed to go free.

Guillaume did this for the sake of his own reputation, because he knew how a gentleman should behave.

The valiant and noble warriors from Champagne, and the French, now took up their shields and jumped into the fray. The richly equipped Germans and the Duke of Saxony's men rushed to join in as well. God, what great blows Guillaume delivered in that valiant company, wherever the fighting was fiercest! Many an opponent was thrown to the ground in this melee, with many a struggle to capture the fallen knights. Men from Lorraine came in through the valley crying: "For Bar! For Bar!" And by Saint Nicolas of Bari, we'll never see anything like this again!

The Count of Boulogne entered the battle with one hundred and forty knights, splendidly equipped, shouting "Onward! Onward!" You can be sure that those in the rear were sorry they weren't in the front ranks! Guillaume, who had been holding back, recognized those cries. He saw Eudes de Ronquerolles, leading the rest. Ah God, what a hard life; those who avoid it are wise indeed! The two knights, as soon as they spied one another, dug in the spurs.[53] They hit with such force that their lances bent and broke, leaving a piece of the shaft embedded in each shield. Night would have done a courteous deed had it ended that joust right then. If you had been there, you would have thought the knights were carpenters. They smashed up shields and ripped the clothes from one another's bodies. Their horses, with the reins tangled in their feet, wandered about the field. My God! What a treasure was there, if anyone had noticed! Not since the time of the Maccabees[54] have helmets taken such blows, for the proudest knights in the Empire and France were fighting.

In the late afternoon, the bright sun moved towards the horizon and quickly set. From every direction you could see prisoners being led off to the camps.[55] There were knights triumphant and knights who had been defeated. Those from France and the Netherlands were so evenly matched that neither had gained one inch of land from the other. The Germans had won great honor for their emperor that day, and the French for their own noble houses. They separated at nightfall without rancor or ill will, as is the rule in such events, but while some were happy, others were very sad. Anyone who has had a bad day will know how they felt.

The emperor watched the tournament until evening. Then, on the advice of his high lords, he left because something needed his attention. That night his noble heart inspired him do a generous deed which greatly augmented his reputation in France. He sent his seneschals around with horses carrying silver and valuable objects to pay the ransom of any who so desired. A king in our times would rather be burned at the stake than make such an offer—it cost at least ten thousand marks. People are still talking about it.

Considering the number of noble lords who went back to their lodgings so much the worse for wear and so dolorous, and the number of prisoners on one side or the other who had lost everything, horses included, except for their doublets, you would have to say that the warrior from Dole, our Guillaume, in possession of three new shields, had made them pay dearly for his helmet. But he had purchased his glory at a high cost in bruises. He returned to his inn black and blue and exhausted. All eyes were upon him. The maidens and ladies and everyone else were waiting at the gates of the town to see what booty the various knights had won. Guillaume brought back nothing but his fame. He wore only a poor doublet; as soon as the fighting was over, he had taken off his armor and given everything, weapons and horses as well, to the heralds. Neither Alexander nor Perceval ever did so many remarkable deeds in a single day.

"Look!" someone said, "There's the one we saw this morning in all his splendor! Now he's riding a nag, and his handsome face is all scratched up."

Someone else said: "Yes, it's the same man; look at his banner!"

Guillaume's appealing face caused any number of ladies to fall in love. Everyone was glad to give him a courteous greeting.

So many torches had been lit, you would have thought all the inns were on fire, when the noble lords arrived with their companions, along with a great many prisoners who had only their doublets to cover the shirts on their backs. They found cloths on the tables, good wines, and meat prepared just the way each of them requested it. Servants brought very welcome warm water so they could wash their necks, bruised from heavy blows, and their handsome faces.

Our wise and valiant Guillaume, his companions, and his hosts enjoyed a very good meal. There were fifteen prisoners also at the table; their ransoms would have to be paid unless Guillaume let them off. There was a good bit less merriment than there had been the night before; noblemen kept arriving, looking for their companions, to ransom them or offer a promise of payment. You can be sure that the valiant Guillaume preferred to enhance his reputation rather than ask a ransom for the knights he had taken himself. A worthy man had only to make a request and it was granted; everyone was pleased.

Things would have gone badly the next morning at Saint-Trond, had it not been for the emperor's thoughtfulness. Thanks to him, more than one man could leave with his head held high who otherwise, reduced to poverty, would have tried to make good his losses by great sin, plundering and looting his hosts. Knights have a hard time of it when they travel from country to country trying to establish their reputations. What can you do? This is an old problem, unlikely ever to be solved. The money the emperor spent on the tournament greatly increased his fame and won him highborn friends from his own kingdom and elsewhere.

It would take me more than all day to tell you what each one did before leaving Saint-Trond. Out of friendship for his hosts, the courtly Guillaume, generous by nature, gave them parting gifts of very fine quality. He sent his servants and his companions back to his house, laden with booty and gifts. Then he returned to court, battered and bruised, and not as rich as when he had left the day before. Don't imagine that he boasted of the fame he had won since then. All the emperor's people were overjoyed to see him. The emperor once again did Guillaume such great honor that nothing seemed enough to show how much he loved him and held him dear.

In the morning they got on their horses and headed for Cologne. Conrad determined to tell Guillaume his thoughts without further delay, being now entirely convinced that he was worthy. The members of Guillaume's household showed him to be a person of great distinction;[56] for his courage alone he deserved a kingdom.

"Come along, my lord Guillaume," he said, "I have something to tell you." Riding together, they left the main road. The emperor took care how he introduced the subject: "A certain nobleman told me that you have a sister who would well be worthy of a great honor, if God bestowed it on her."

"Nothing could make me happier than that, Sire!" replied Guillaume instantly.

The king said, "On my soul, they say she is very lovely, and still a maiden."

"Sire, that is true."

"What is her name?"

(Ah God! Why did he ask? The name henceforth will be written on his heart, never to leave him. She is called the fair Liénor. The emperor thought how pleasant it was to hear other people speak of the one you love. For this reason he didn't dare to say her name himself, for fear of being found out.)[57]

"There is no more beautiful lady from here to the Tiber, and her name is Liénor."

"That's a very beautiful name," the emperor said; "it's a long time since I've heard it."

"Really?" responded Guillaume. "It's not unusual where I come from."

The emperor said, "I've thought of nothing but your sister for three days. I have heard that no lady in the world is as intelligent or as beautiful as she, and what's more, that she is a virgin. So if it be God's will, I want to make her my lady and my wife, and she will be queen and ruler over all the women in the Empire."

"You can make fun of her all you like," said Guillaume, "but just the same, by her beauty and noble birth, she would indeed be worthy of the most glorious destiny God could bestow on her. I'll leave her marriage to God, to arrange as He sees fit. But I'll tell you this: if you had any concern for my feelings, you wouldn't have distressed me by suggesting such a thing. Even for her weight in gold, it could never be."

"Why is that?"

"Because the noblemen of your Empire would say it was nonsense. Do what your counselors advise. Ask for the hand of the French king's daughter, and leave this orphan girl alone.[58] Believe me, I love her more than any queen in the world. She is my hope, my life, my treasure, my happiness. Any woman would be overjoyed to resemble her in the least detail. When her hair is unveiled, there is no one so beautiful."

Guillaume's praise of his sister left Conrad deep in thought. "Listen to me," he said, "I have to have her; it can't be otherwise, if God keeps me from harm. And to put an end to your doubts, I'll tell you my plan. The noble princes and barons of my realm have begged and advised me a hundred times to get married, so that if I died or went overseas on a pilgrimage there would be a king of my lineage to rule after me. If they had another king, someone not raised as they were, he might not treat them as well. So I'll do what they wish. As soon as we're in Cologne, I'll have my knights see that proclamations and letters are sent to all the barons of Germany, high or low, so that not one will fail to attend my assembly in Mainz on the first of May. Then I will ask them to show their gratitude and love by granting me a gift. I know they won't refuse. And as soon as they have been good enough to agree, I'll make them swear to it, so they can't go back on their word. Then I'll tell them my heart's desire is to make your sister my wife, for no one else is as worthy of the honor of being empress."

"Sire," said Guillaume, "a thousand thanks. Now I see that you really meant what you said."

With his hands joined in homage, he said he would always be grateful that Conrad had opened his heart to him and let him know what he intended to do. They very much enjoyed all the rest of the day. They didn't go back to the road, but rode over the fields.

The king said: "Do you know this song?"

> Whatever they say, it's madness
> to think a new love I'd start;
> her harshness gives more gladness
> than the gift of another's heart.
> So I'm content to serve,
> where honor has no place,
> vile traitors who don't deserve
> their chances to see her face.

There was nothing to trouble them all the way to Cologne. A count and the Duke of Burgundy came to meet the emperor, and escorted him through the city to do him honor; many princes and highborn men were present.

Right after supper Conrad had the letters and messages written and sealed in heavy gold. Young men who could run faster than horses were ordered to carry them throughout his lands.

The King's seneschal held land near Aachen and had not been at court since Guillaume arrived. Now he came to Cologne, with more than twenty valiant knights. The emperor gave him a hard time about his absence: "Do other seneschals take so long to get to court? In the good old days, King Louis of France had Bouchard le Veautre; it seems to me that he was fonder of court life than you are!"

The king teased him this way for quite a while. The seneschal just laughed; he was used to Conrad's ways. His own position in the household was second only to the king's. In matters of importance everyone deferred to his opinion.

The emperor spent the next two weeks in Cologne and at his castles nearby. The seneschal, much in favor, was constantly in his presence. He saw how things were: Conrad had such esteem for the young Guillaume that he would do absolutely nothing without him. In the house or out in the woods and fields, the two were always together.

The seneschal's shield had a brass knob and bore the coat-of-arms of King Arthur's seneschal. Kay was no match for him in wickedness![59] He soon was extremely jealous of Guillaume, and kept close to the two men, plotting, trying to find out the reason for their friendship. One day, when he was eavesdropping as usual, he heard Guillaume say something about his sister. The emperor responded warmly and exchanged Guillaume's belt for one of his own. They were leaning against a windowsill after dinner, overlooking an orchard. The singing of birds inspired Conrad to make up this song[60]:

> When the orchard trees are once again in leaf,
> the grass is green and color in the rose,
> and early in the morning I can hear
> the nightingale as through the woods it goes,
> against love's power what could I oppose?
> There is no other treasure that I seek,
>   but love,
> and only love can bring an end to grief.
>
> Because the scandalmongers lie in wait,
> there cannot be true love exempt from fear.
> Surely she would no longer hesitate,
> were there a way to show her I am here
> to serve her as she will. I tolerate
> those whose vain words malign what I revere,
>   true love,
> for in love returned, love's sorrows disappear.

It was an unlucky impulse that made him sing those two verses, and he suffered for it later, thanks to the seneschal's vindictiveness. When that traitor heard the song, he thought, "Now I understand! It's not valor that wins him such favor, it's his sister." But why should that matter to the seneschal? His position was secure; he just couldn't stand any happiness in which he had no share. Insanely jealous, he left them and went to his lodgings.

No thief ever put so much effort into devising a plan as the seneschal did into figuring out how to destroy their friendship. He seized on a fantastic scheme. To accomplish his treacherous purpose, he had to go to Guillaume's home. He went to a great deal of trouble to keep his intention secret. He let it be known that he had to take care of some business in his own lands; he would leave more than half of his men with the king and would soon return. He hoped very much that it wouldn't be inconvenient for the king to have someone else take charge of his affairs for a short time.

Accompanied by two men, he slipped away from the castle. As he rode along, with the devil urging him on, he thought of one lie after another, imagining how he would talk to the maiden, giving her many greetings from her brother. He would tell her that his lord, the emperor, had commanded him to call on her mother to find out how things were with her and if there was anything she needed. The emperor desired her well-being just as much as her own son did. In this way he would learn what their life at home was like. He was sure to find out something to further his plan.

It took them a full five days to get to the home of the lady whose beauty was as superior to all others as summer's warmth is to winter's cold. They rode rapidly until they were close to their destination. Then the seneschal sent one of his squires ahead on a fast, sturdy horse—neither sore nor lame—to announce his arrival. The young man galloped right up to the house.

The lady, who was always impeccably dressed, was outside calling her young peacocks. The young man dismounted in the courtyard and let his horse wander about. He went straight up to her, in a mannerly way, and said: "Lady, I am a messenger from the emperor's seneschal. As a sign of his esteem for your son, he is coming here to see you."

"Friend, that is very kind of him," she said; "I give him my thanks." Turning to her servants she said, "Hurry and prepare the beds upstairs."

You should have seen the great numbers of coverlets they threw on the beds, quilts beautifully embroidered with coats of arms. The lady drew a flowing fur-trimmed cloak around her shoulders. Its tie-cords weren't plain, but made of fine silk.[61] Soon the seneschal, goaded on by the devil, arrived and dismounted in the courtyard with his two companions. A large number of servants ran out to take the horses. The lady, who knew how to treat a guest, hurried to greet him, saying he was most welcome.

"Lady, first of all, I bring you the good wishes of my lord and then those of the most worthy knight ever born of woman."

"Sir, God's blessing on the emperor and on you. May God protect and favor him, great ruler that he is!" She then sent for some knights who had just gone into town to play chess at the home of a priest. She didn't ask the seneschal right away if he would like something to drink, because she expected that he would stay the night. Leading him by the hand into the fine house, whose floors were strewn with rushes, she offered him a cushioned seat near a bed. "Have the horses stabled," she said.

"Lady," said he, "we can't stay. The officials of Besançon have asked me to hear an important case tomorrow morning. But I would have been very remiss, and would have heard many reproaches at court, had I passed this way without calling on you. Your son, whom I greatly admire, would have been very much displeased. He is a man of such quality that the emperor would do anything for him.[62] The two of us are companions-in-arms; we fight as one man."

The lady, weeping tears of joy, said how happy she was to hear it. "Really, my lord, you must have something to eat."

"Unfortunately, my lady, I can't stay, but if possible I'd like to meet your daughter." (I'll bet he would!) "Where is she?"

"In her room with her maid."

"And won't she come down?"

"Certainly not, I'm sorry to say. I hope you don't think I'm making this up, but the fact is no man is allowed to see her when her brother isn't home."

"I'm very sorry to hear it, my lady, but if that's the way it is, I do understand. I desire to have your love as long as I live, and want you to have this ring as a token of mine."

The lady did not refuse, lest he think her discourteous. The gold in the ring must have weighed five *besants*, and the stone, a bright red ruby, was extremely valuable. "Many thanks, my lord," said she, "I will cherish your gift."

Before he mounted his horse, which a servant had been holding at the doorway, she told him all kinds of things about herself and her life. A beautiful present can work like magic to make us say and do things we really shouldn't. She told him about the rose on her daughter's thigh. "No man who is capable of speech will ever see so great a marvel as the crimson rose on her soft white thigh. Believe me, you couldn't hear of a greater marvel." She described its beauty in great detail and exactly how big it was.

The thief was intent on finding out all about the rose. When he had learned all that he could without actually seeing it, he said, "It's getting late." He left the lady, assuring her of his eternal devotion. Poor foolish woman! Better she hadn't lived to see this day.

When he had taken leave of her, he mounted his jet black horse: "Lady, farewell! I'll always be at your service."

"Dear sir, may Saint Peter the Apostle go with you and your companions." And so, as if duty called him, the traitor, the murderous thief, departed. His visit brought great misfortune to him and to others.

Now let's return to the emperor. While his perfidious seneschal was traveling about, Conrad stayed in his castles, hunting with dogs and birds, accompanied by his knights. At bedtime he often called for a minstrel. His chamberlains had a marvelous little one, good enough to eat,[63] called Cupelin. He played this song for the emperor every morning:

> I gave her the white fur-lined vest,
> but it was Thierion she loved best.
> Ha! Ha! just as I thought!
> To me that shepherdess no pleasure brought.

The king really liked this young fellow. And then there was Hugh, who came to the court from Brasseuse, near Ognon. The emperor insisted that he teach him a French dance performed by girls under the elms at Trumilly, known for its delightful parties. Conrad asked him to play on the vielle and sing this song about the lovely Marguerite, who performs the new songs so well[64]:

> She's from Oissery
> and never forgets
> to go to a party.
> So charming is she,
> such games never yet
> were played under trees.
> She wears a fine chaplet
> of roses still dewy;
> her young face glows prettily,
> gray eyes speak sincerely,
> she wears her fine jewelry
> to cause other girls regret.

Everyone said, "Good for her!"

"Not that our own ladies suffer in comparison," said the king, "don't you agree?"[65]

And so the worthy emperor passed the time until the seneschal returned. The evening before that happened was the best and most delightful that Conrad had ever enjoyed. As for Guillaume, he had never been so happy. He couldn't wait for the assembly at Mainz, and kept thinking of the great honor he expected to gain from it. But first he will have to drink a bitter brew; his lineage, his high-born family, even his knightly virtues won't help him. God! How sad it is when a man's rise in the world costs him unbearable pain and suffering! What did the seneschal think he would gain by plotting against Guillaume? Few men have been so treacherous![66]

While the emperor was enjoying himself, the seneschal arrived at court, where his friends were delighted to see him. Before he had even opened his mouth, Conrad said: "Well, seneschal, here you are back already!" The two began to talk, and the seneschal lied to the king; believe me, here was one who could get the goat and the cabbages home together.[67] He knew very well how to pull the wool over someone's eyes.

"Seneschal, I want to have a long talk with you."

"Sire," he said, "I'm completely at your service."

Now we'll see things start to happen.[68] The two of them went out on a balcony away from the other knights.

"Seneschal," Conrad said, "I think we should head for Mainz right away. May first is upon us and the nobles of my realm will be waiting for me there. Last year you and everyone else kept trying to get me to marry. I've thought about it a lot and realize that, at my age, I really should. My youth might have excused my frivolous heart, but I would rightly be criticized if I continued that way. I can't be so irresponsible any more. For once, I'm willing to yield to my advisors."

"Sire, this does you great honor; surely God has inspired your words. If the knights of your realm can now be certain that you want to take a wife, nothing could make them happier. Does your heart lean toward any one woman more than another?"

"Ah! Believe me, the one I love is as superior to other women as alabaster is to ordinary stone."

"Is the noble lady French? Is she the king's daughter or his sister?" (Ah! How he's leading him on!) "What will you gain from it? Will she bring you lands and money, alliances?"

"A man acquires land and wealth enough if he weds a wise, noble, and beautiful virgin."

"There aren't many like that," said the cruel and wicked man.

The king replied, "That may well be. But since God has created this one, and has given her every imaginable gift, why wouldn't she be as worthy of a kingdom as the daughter of the king of Scotland or Ireland?"[69]

The seneschal then asked who she was, since everyone would find out at the assembly.

"True enough," he replied. "She's the sister of my friend Guillaume de Dole. Whoever saw him riding yesterday would have had to admire him."

"He is indeed an outstanding knight. No doubt about it. He is second to none in your kingdom. And no woman can rival his sister in elegance and dress. If beauty alone could make a woman honorable, she would certainly take the prize. But there is something else which makes the marriage impossible. If your princes and high officials knew about it, no matter how much good they saw in her, and even though you love her, they would never allow such an alliance."

"Why? Her beauty is considered to have no peer."

"So they say."

"By my soul, you can't tolerate anything good! What problem could there be? The lovely orphan Liénor is the right age, virtuous, and worthy in all respects."

As much as the one sang her praises, the other, with his malicious assertions, tried to undermine them.

"I know of no hidden vice, nor any reason why I should delay. I'm not going to hold it against her that she's not sister to England's king! I have enough wealth and land for as long as I live. Seneschal, you're either jealous or just ill-natured. You insist on seeing the worst in everything. If you convinced me to give her up, that would be a great sin."

He pressed him so hard that the seneschal finally made his outrageous claim: he said he had had her virginity, and as proof, he described the rose on her thigh. The king was stunned. He crossed himself and after a while he said sadly, "Never did a king lose his queen before the chessboard was even set up. But we'll have to bear it, if it's God's will. Make sure that her brother, who is responsible for her, never gets wind of it. We'll still start for Mainz tomorrow morning."

And so he set off at the first light of dawn, although a long day of travel was most unwelcome. "God," he said, "what an unlucky maiden! I'll never forgive the man who told me she lost her honor. Only two and a half months ago, how far I was from imagining anything like this—I never would have believed it! The traitor who took her virginity truly hates others' good fortune. No doubt many will suffer for it before long."

Leaving the main road, he traveled all alone across the fields, very sad and forlorn, resting his hand on the saddlebow. He remembered some fine verses by Gace Brulé which did him a lot of good: a worthy man gains nothing by being doleful to no purpose. He started to sing a bit of the song out loud.

> You're out of your mind,
> as long as you still care
> for your wife or your lover,

> if you try to discover
> what she does when you're not there.
> Your love won't recover
> if your jealousy lays bare
> what you'd rather not discover.

He rode along joylessly until he arrived in Mainz, where the citizens showed him great honor and respect. Everyone in the royal party had lodgings perfectly suited to their taste; no need to ask Saint Julian for help![70] Though the emperor was grateful for the reception he was given by his subjects, the court was saddened to observe his obvious distress. God, how fond he had been of Guillaume only three days ago! What had happened? Guillaume didn't dare to ask. He was wise enough to realize that lovesickness couldn't account for it.

One day, the emperor was in his palace with just a few people. He summoned the noble Guillaume, to whom Nature had doled out good looks, brains, and valor. "Dear friend," he said, "come into the orchard and chat with me." Ignoring the others, they went out together, arm in arm; the seneschal watched them go. Guillaume touched the clasp of his cloak and began to smile. His lord the emperor said, "By the loyalty you owe me, what's so funny?"

"I'm laughing because of a prophecy which will very soon come true. No wonder, since everything happens because God wishes it to. The other day I was honored to receive from you a letter bearing your seal on which was engraved a handsome king on horseback. My sister gave me this brooch and I gave her the seal.[71] Then she said, with that charming laugh of hers, 'Dear brother, I'm delighted that I have a king in my household!'"

"That was a happy thought, and indeed it almost came true. I had hoped to have her as my wife, but now I realize that this is impossible."

"I'd go out of my mind if I believed that![72] But it's base of you to make fun of a noble woman."

"My barons would never allow the marriage."

"Well, God did not reject her! He has taken such good care of her that never, until now, has she known any lack of wealth and honor."

The emperor hated to see him so doleful: "Things are quite different from what you think. She's been been keeping bad company and has lost her senses."

"Lost her senses! She hasn't been tied up or had her head shaved! Her beautiful blond hair is a gift from God!"

"A man told me something for which he has absolute proof. However he feels about her, he certainly admires her, except that she's not a virgin."

"In other words, she's raving mad! You sell me on the idea of this marriage and then publicly dishonor me and make unfounded accusations against my sister! If God meant for her to have the honor of being your wife, he would never have allowed her to be mistreated, demeaned, or violated, or (may His holy mother be praised) lose anything whatsoever!"

"Do you know what makes it a sure thing? She has that rose on her thigh; there has never been such a beautiful thing on a rosebush or on a shield."

With this the king prevailed; Liénor's brother could no longer blame him. Guillaume was in such distress he almost fainted. He had believed that no one knew about the rose except his mother and himself. He drew his fresh new cloak over his head and went to his lodgings.

The emperor, with sorrow in his heart, returned alone to the palace. He didn't know how he could be sociable, no matter how insistent and eloquent the requests for his company might be. But he knew he would have to resign himself to his situation. He would have avenged himself on Love, if he could—he had lost his heart just by hearing about the maiden whose name was so beautiful. Sighing, weeping, and terribly angry, he complained of Love's cruel treachery in the verses of this song.

> Tell me for what reason or what crime,
> Love, you have banished me so far away
> that I cannot even hope there'll come a time
> when someone will take pity when I pray.
> I view my long devotion with regret,
> if my reward is only bitter pain.
> Never, Love, have I reproached you yet
> for anything, but now I do complain,
> and say that you have slain me for no crime.

Now this powerful man, this emperor, this lofty lord, was pensive and doleful because of the love he felt for the maiden; pain had replaced all joy in his heart. And as for the worthy Guillaume, he pounded his fists together and struck his own body in his grief, saying, "I'd sooner have died than had this happen."

His friends all came to see him, and everyone in his household was so disconcerted they didn't know what to do. Tearing at his handsome face, he groaned: "How miserable and dolorous I am! From very high I have truly fallen very low."

Who would be hard-hearted enough to hear his lament without pity? Who would not grieve to see a man so elegant and so handsome in such a state?

"My God!" said the Germans he had abandoned,[73] "He's dying! His mouth is hanging open as if he were crazy!"

One of Guillaume's nephews,[74] coming back from riding in the fields, heard the noise in his uncle's lodgings as he went down the main street. As you would imagine, he didn't delay but quickly dismounted and went to Guillaume. Unsmiling, he asked what was going on. His uncle replied, "I swear that no one, unless he guesses it, will ever find out from me."

The young man realized that it must have something to do with another knight or with a lady—so worthy a man would never have carried on like this over some material loss. "Uncle, tell me the truth; has someone brought you news of my lady or of your sister? Has there been a death among our friends?"

"Nephew," said he, "It was that vile whore, that faithless, rotten—"

"By the Lord's five wounds, who are you talking about?"

"That slut Liénor has disgraced us! She has so abandoned virtue that everyone has turned against me."[75]

"Tell me what happened."

Guillaume told him all about how Liénor had dishonored him. On the first of May she would have been an empress! Her extraordinary beauty had made the emperor want to marry her! His grief caused heartfelt tears to run down his face: "But she lost her virginity—that's what has made me so miserable! That's why there won't be a marriage!"

"How did he find out?"

"He told me about the rose she has on her thigh. How can I be avenged? All I can do is weep."

"Uncle, she'll die for this. If she doesn't do it herself, I'll kill her with my own two hands. Women will always play fast and loose and dishonor their friends. This is the devil's work; Liénor hates nothing so much as honor if it stands in her way. What a great shame that a worthy and valiant man like you showed such affection for her. My dear uncle, don't make two tragedies out of one! Dear God, what would people say if you died for such a reason? Her behavior is disgusting; I'm ashamed to say she's lived up to her doleful name! I'm leaving right now to avenge you and put an end to your grief!"

Without saying another word, he went to his horse and mounted. He took the road straight to Dole; he was outraged for his uncle and everyone would know it when he got there. He was weeping when he left; he and his uncle exchanged no farewells.

The nephew left and the uncle stayed behind. The emperor and many others went often to visit him. Fine jewels and lovely gifts were not lying idle. Once or twice each day, the emperor sent someone to see how Guillaume was doing. Whenever he had any good news of him, he of course was greatly cheered. One day he remembered the lovely lady of Dole whom he had heard so much about; he had never laid eyes on her.[76] He recalled a beautiful poem by Renaut de Sablé, and his gentle heart sought consolation in singing:

> Now I shall sing no more,
> so heavy is my woe.
> All that I ask Love for
> is death, to let me go.
> Never will any one
> serve her as I have done,
> and that she treats me so,
> the whole world must deplore.
>
> Alas! what I said before
> was raving mad; my wild
> heart had set its course
> to play the foolish child.
> Great is my remorse,
> my Lady, but I know
> how late it comes—that's why
> I only deserve to die.

The fires of love were still burning. "Ah," said he, "fair Liénor! How the seneschal has betrayed me! All this pain and suffering comes from my love of you and your brother."

And in truth, the emperor still wanted to marry her, but no longer dared to hope. It could never be.

The nephew had already left many valleys and hills behind on his way to Dole; night and day he goaded his horse, and didn't stop even once until he arrived. He dismounted in the courtyard and a young man ran up, delighted to see him. Guillaume's nephew drew his sword and ran to the great hall. God grant that someone stop him from doing something crazy! In the doorway he cried out, "Where is the whore, the vile slut who threw away a chance to be queen and empress?" He tripped on a piece of wood and fell down, sword in hand. A servant, who had just skewered a goose between two ducks, and who was neither a weakling nor a coward, jumped up and grabbed him. Now he couldn't do much harm, except by talking. Another fellow collared him and the two of them held him fast.

His aunt, shocked and dismayed, rushed up, shouting, "Holy Mary, help us!"

"Old woman, shame on you! You should be run through and through for being so careless!"

"For heaven's sake, dear nephew, what are you talking about?"

"Liénor! If I can get hold of her, I swear I'll kill her with my own two hands!"

He forced his way to her room. His cousin heard him shouting; she opened her door and came out. At the sight of her he yelled, "Ah! Here you are, disloyal Liénor, I've come looking for you!"

"We'll have to tie him up; he's lost his mind!"

"That's a lie! I know perfectly well what I'm saying. Only a week ago Tuesday I left my uncle in Mainz either dead or dying. May the faithless woman who shamed him die a most horrible death. She could have had the greatest of honors, but instead she brought him low. Look at her with that beautiful hair of hers! I'd like to take my sword and chop it all off!"

"Dear nephew, tell me! What happened? What on earth has my beautiful daughter done to deserve such a punishment?"

"She has brought terrible shame on herself. Her brother's valor and the fame of her great beauty had so impressed the emperor that he wanted to marry her. But now he won't, because she's not a virgin."

When the mother and the daughter heard this, which they both knew to be totally untrue, they were grief-stricken and wept hot tears. "Nephew," said the lady, "may my body be torn to pieces and my daughter drowned before my very eyes, if ever you heard such nonsense!"

"You'd better not swear to that; we all know it's true because she has that rose near the top of her plump white thigh, may it burn in hell!"

"This is all my fault! I'm the one who should be punished!" said the mother.

At the thought of her son so very close to death, she closed her eyes and fainted dead away. Virtue always makes the devil jealous. The young man realized that he could gain nothing by making a scene. Seeing his elderly aunt being kissed and hugged in her daughter's arms, he felt such pity that he put his sword back in its scabbard.[77]

While her mother lay there unconscious, Liénor said: "May God reward each of us—the seneschal and ourselves—as we deserve. My mother showed him such fine hospitality! Who could have imagined that harm would come to us as a result?"[78]

The mother gave a sigh and opened her eyes, which were full of tears. "Alas," she said, "I don't want to live any longer. The seneschal has brought me to despair. I saw no harm in telling him what I did, and to think he would act this way when he said he loved me and gave me a ring! He has asked too great a price for his gift, if it costs me the life of my son!"

"Dear Mother, before the end of April, which isn't far away, I will have exposed his wickedness and his lie. I'll make him admit that everything he told the emperor was untrue. I put all my trust in God. I've done nothing wrong and have no reason to be afraid."

Although she seemed very confident, in her heart she was deeply troubled. She prayed to the Holy Spirit to comfort her and her mother, and all their household; everyone was grief-stricken because of her misfortune. If by the seneschal's trick she lost the chance of becoming empress, he would have destroyed them all. "Lady, send for some horses. I'm going to court to see my brother; he must not die for such a reason. People have always preferred to say wicked things rather than good ones. But believe me when I tell you that I will return rejoicing. Our Lord fed his people with five loaves and two fishes, and He will save our honor since we are truly in the right." She then had two worthy gentlemen sent for; they would accompany her.[79] Thanks to her clear-headedness, her mother and everyone present began to feel better. The nephew, who had been so upset and so hard to calm down, spent the day making preparations for the trip.

Two beautiful coffers were filled with Liénor's clothes—an astonishing number for an orphan maiden. She also had many beautiful jewels, having already prepared her whole wedding trousseau. Liénor was the most capable of young women; this is clear and will become even clearer. At her departure, early the next morning, there was much kissing and crying: "Dear daughter, may Saint Honoré be with you, wherever you go."

"Dear Mother, may God, in whom I place all my trust, watch over you."

The maiden prepared to mount her horse, and no one who witnessed the parting of mother and daughter could keep from crying, even if he had to borrow the tears. Everyone was quite overwhelmed by grief. Weeping, each one of them commended her by name to God's care. The mother begged her nephew to take care of Liénor. Hot tears rolled down her face. Ah God! Would that the seneschal had yet to be born!

The two knights who accompanied Liénor sadly left the house. The ones who remained helped the mother to bed. She truly believed she had lost all joy and delight forever.

"She takes all our happiness with her," said those who followed Liénor to the town gates. With immense grief they commended the maiden to God (who took good care of her) and she them. Then she left; may God watch over her! And He will; I know it for a fact.

Now it would be good to see how her brother is getting along. Nothing could comfort him; words of consolation had no effect. Every day the emperor came to visit or sent someone else in his place. He told Guillaume whatever he could think of to raise his spirits. One evening the good and noble king went to see him after supper. Conrad was alone, except for one knight and Jouglet. They listened to a young man sing a good song by the Vidame of Chartres. It seemed to the emperor, as he rode along, that no one had ever sung it better:

> When we have once again enjoyed the spring,
> and summer in its beauty starts to glow,
> and to its own true nature every thing
> returns, unless, unworthy, it's too slow;
> then, to find some comfort, I must sing
> the sorrow of a cruel love affair,
> the hopes that have condemned me to despair.
>
> I have no reason to conceal my grief.
> Why did I ever see her lovely face?
> Now, for my suffering, there's no relief;
> I've felt what nothing ever can erase.
> I'm so completely captive to her grace,
> her gentle heart alone can bring me peace,
> or, through excess of pain, my life will cease.

The king said: "Jouglet, this song must have been written just for me."

The last two weeks of April went by. The noblemen of the realm assembled in Mainz and their pleasure in being there was very apparent.

Two days before the first of May, the merrymaking had reached an astonishing pitch. All the citizens went out to the woods in the middle of the night. Mainz was famous as a place where you could have a really good time. The next morning, when it was fully daylight, they returned with their leafy green May tree, laden with flowers and gladioli, the most beautiful ever seen. They went in procession, rejoicing, through the city, while two young noblemen sang:

> Down there by the sea,
> friends, let's sing merrily!
> We'll dance with fair ladies—
>   my heart is gay—
> friends, let's sing merrily
>   in honor of May!

They sang it through to the end, and then boughs were carried upstairs as decorations, and flowers and greenery were tossed out of the windows down to the pavement. Thus they did honor to the day and the noble assembly.

It was truly a prodigal display of riches! All up and down, the streets had been hung with fine cloth, and the gables of all the houses were draped in expensive cendal and oriental silks, ermine, and gold brocade. Everything in sight was richly decorated.

The fair one, who had left her home feeling so sad, was thinking very different thoughts from those of the people in Mainz. She traveled along until, early one morning, she at last saw the city. That day she spoke very directly to her two knights[80]: "If you don't object, I would like my nephew to go on ahead of us now and arrange for our lodging; I want it to be as far as possible from where his uncle, my brother, is staying."

"Lady," they said, "let one of these squires go with him, since someone has to come back to show us the way."

The nephew then left his aunt. He and the squire rode off into the rich and beautiful city, taking the side streets in search of lodgings for the maiden. God provided them with a worthy and courteous hostess, one of two townswomen who were just returning from morning mass. She took them to her house, which was in a somewhat secluded street and had every comfort. She showed them a gaily decorated and quite lovely room, and then the stables. It was truly a charming place with its garden and well. "Gentlemen," said she, "I can't show the place other than it is."

"Lady, it has everything we need. May God bring you happiness this day!"

One of them jumped on his horse and went to find the others. The inn was lovely and pleasant, though it was a very simple place. Just as the young man went through the city gate, he encountered the others and told them the good news about the lodging arranged for them. It was exactly what they had asked for. The two knights led the noble maiden there; she had pulled her hood down over her face. They helped her dismount in the courtyard and the hostess ran down the stairs to wish her welcome.

She took Liénor by the hand and led her to her room. Liénor asked why such a great crowd of people were there for the first of May. Her hostess told her what she had heard people saying: their lord, the emperor, was intending to take a wife. Therefore, he had sent word throughout the kingdom for all his noble lords to assemble. It was only right and reasonable that he confer with them. The fair one said: "Now may God advise him, since He knows what is best. It would give me pleasure to see all this, if it weren't for something very sad."

Tears clearer than rose water ran down her face. A great wrong had been committed, and if God didn't perform a miracle, Liénor might lose both her honor and her brother. She wept, for her heart was heavy with the sorrow she felt for her mother. She called her nephew and her knights in order to get their advice: "My lords," she said, "which of your servants do you consider most capable? I need him to carry a message for me to a nobleman at court."

One of the knights said that a certain young man was discreet and able: "I can assure you that he'll carry out your task very well."

She sent for the messenger right away, and asked her nephew, the knights, and their servants to leave the room. To the handsome and elegant young man she said: "Take this brooch to the seneschal for me, along with this embroidered cloth belt and this little purse. They all show the same emblem, and inside the purse is a beautiful emerald ring; make sure no one sees it. Tell the seneschal that these things were sent to him by the Chatelaine of Dijon; it was for him that the little birds and fish were embroidered. Dear friend, pay close attention to what I'm telling you. Say that you left Dijon on Tuesday to visit him. This is your lucky day, if you do the job well."

"If God lets no accident befall me, you can be sure I will."

Said the maiden, "I know that he courted her, but she never wanted to give him a promise of love. Then one day she realized that she had been behaving very badly. Therefore, her message to him is that if he wants her to receive him, he must wear the sash she's sending him under his shirt, on his bare skin. Once you've seen him put it on, tell him that with this ring, which she took off her own little finger, she accedes to his wishes, and that she is heartsick at having so often refused him. A maiden who used to carry their messages told me all about this.[81] My dear friend, do keep your wits about you: if he tries to draw you out, just tell him that she asked you not to say any more, except that she is eager to see him, and will soon arrange a way. You'll find him at his lodgings, or else at the assembly with the king."

He replied: "Don't worry; I'll look until I find him." He left immediately; may God be with him and bring him back safely!

The lady in whose house Liénor was staying came back with the others when the maiden sent for them. Liénor told the knights to put on the clothes of violet silk lined with squirrel fur she had recently had them buy. To go with their elegant new costumes, she gave each of them white gloves and a narrow belt embroidered with coats of arms in gold.

Her nephew laid out what Liénor would wear.[82] Her cloak was marvelously beautiful, made of blue silk and lined with the whitest and finest ermine you can imagine. Over her white shift, embroidered with flowers, she wore only a tunic made of green cendal silk lined with fur. Her hips were low, her waist was slim, and her lovely, firm breasts pressed against the silk. Nature had fashioned her with the greatest care; God and the Holy Spirit willing, whatever the seneschal said will turn against him. Her neck was long and smooth, white, just as it should be, without any sores or wrinkles. For a maiden so sad and suffering, she was very well able to dress and adorn herself. To show off her neck, she closed the top of her shift with an exquisitely worked and finely made gold brooch; she placed it rather low so that an opening, one finger wide, gave a glimpse of her breasts, white as snow on the branches. This made her look even lovelier.

While she was tying on her wimple and fastening her belt (the gold of its buckle was worth more than twenty-five pounds), the messenger, who was neither a fool nor drunk, didn't tarry in accomplishing his mission. He found the seneschal in the midst of the assembly. He spoke to him courteously and, as they conversed, managed to lead him out of the palace and close to a high wall. When he saw that they were quite alone and safe from prying eyes, he unfastened his cloak, and said: "My lord, I am a messenger from the wisest and finest of ladies: the Chatelaine of Dijon. I came here as fast as I could; from the time I left on Tuesday, I didn't stop once to rest along the way. Through me she sends you word that she accedes to your wishes, in token of which she sends you this ring and this belt."

When the gifts had been taken out of their wrapping, "Dear friend," said the seneschal, "may God give my lady joy and happiness."

He looked at the brooch, the ring, and the belt with great care, and also the purse; he was overcome by a very strange feeling. It seemed to him a miracle that she had thus remembered him. Whatever the explanation, he greatly prized the gifts; his pleasure shone in his eyes and lit up his whole face. The messenger knew just how to play his rôle. He was so persuasive that he managed to talk the seneschal into putting the belt on under his shirt, around his waist. The seneschal pulled it so tight that his skin became quite red. Next he wanted to pin on the brooch. The messenger had to fake a yawn to prevent himself from bursting out laughing. Said he: "She asked me to tell you to keep it in the purse, so that no one will recognize it and die of jealousy."

"She speaks wisely and well, dear friend. Have you found lodgings yet? As you can see, we're so busy here I can't take care of you myself; but upon my soul these gifts are worth more to me than one hundred pounds! Tonight, when I'm free, we'll talk. But go now, and have a fur-lined costume made for yourself: a good cloak, a long tunic, and a sleeveless one. The bill will be taken care of, even if it's a hundred *sous* or more. I don't know what else to say, but go now, and take good care of yourself; I have to get back to the king."

They had soon taken their leave of one another. The squire was overjoyed to have so totally deceived the seneschal; his words had not fallen on deaf ears. Now he hurried back to Liénor. He found her so splendidly attired that no one could compare to her in beauty.

"Well, my friend, what news do you bring me from the court?"

"There are a lot of Flemish people there, short ones and tall ones, and a great crush of noblemen."

Ah! She could hardly wait to find out the real news! In secret he told her how he had managed. He had done even better than she had asked, and her gentle heart beat faster in her breast, such joy did she feel. "May God never show kindness to me or my friends if I do not show you my gratitude for this service; it has won you my esteem."

To those of her companions who were accustomed to court society she said: "My lords, let's go to this great assembly; if we miss it today, we won't see anything like it for a long time."

Servants quickly brought their beautiful horses. Hers was a dappled grey with a lovely mane; the saddle and bridle were as splendid as one could wish and the saddle blanket, which reached all the way to the ground, was of fine English cloth, slashed to show its lining of yellow silk. The bow and cantle of the saddle were not made of wood, but of ivory inlaid with enamels. If need be, one could mount a horse with less attractive gear! I don't know why I'm going on and on, so I'll simply say that before she got to the assembly more than a hundred people had noticed her. The horse was beautiful and well-bred, and its accoutrements most attractive.

Before the noble maiden mounted, she very graciously expressed her thanks to her hostess by giving her a ring set with two emeralds. Not since the days of Bertha of the Big Feet, or the death of Olivier's sister Aude, had there been a woman so truly worthy of praise.[83] Her knights quickly took a panel from one of their cloaks and helped Liénor to mount her horse;[84] then they mounted their own. They arranged her clothing so that it wouldn't get in her way as she rode. Needless to say, she waved goodbye to her hostess as she left.

A maiden so attired, and so accompanied, so ingenious, so determined, can certainly go to court and present herself to a king. As she rode along, surrounded by her knights, the people, one and all, wished her well. She had draped the panels of her cloak in front of her so that it framed the upper part of her body. And, even better, she had left her face uncovered. She kept one hand on the tie-cord of her cloak; the other held the reins. All those to whom she spoke said that she had the voice of an angel. All the rich townspeople of the money-changing district[85] came out to greet her, and all of them praised in their hearts her simplicity and her modest demeanor. They said, "You won't find her equal in all the kingdom of France."

A pickpocket would have had an easy time with those who followed the maiden, lost in thought. The horses of her knights had sweet-sounding bells attached to their harnesses. Dressed in squirrel fur and miniver, highborn ladies came out on their balconies; they would have loved to have one of her smiles.

As she rode along greeting them, the townswomen said, "What is the emperor doing, still looking for a wife? Good heavens! All he has to do is take this lady!" Exactly! The fear that he wouldn't was what worried Liénor.

As you know, the May tree had already been brought to Mainz. Now let's see what was happening at the palace. Minstrels from many lands were trying to earn a living singing songs and stories there. The beautiful Doete from Troyes was singing this little song:

When it's the season
for green grass to grow,
then, with good reason,
toward joy we should go.
    I was alone,
    sounds I'd known
    filled the air
    all around.
And there
a smiling girl I found
with sheep in her care,
and she was singing, all alone,
    having fun;
    a gentle one,
    wind lifting her hair,
    so blond and fair.

And a singer from Châlons, beautifully dressed all in green, offered this:

This suffering, this torment—love is its name,
but other people know love otherwise;
and so my heart has reason to complain:
there's only cruelty in her replies.
And I say, "Alas! When comes the end of pain?"
But may Jesus not allow my woes to cease
until, when they depart, my joys increase.

From a room where the barons were gathered, the emperor heard this song. How different were his thoughts from theirs! He was so deep in sorrow he didn't know what he was saying or doing; anyone could tell from his face that he hadn't cheered up one bit in the last two weeks.

The maiden crossed herself when she entered the court. At least three hundred people (never imagining her agitation) pointed at her, and they all said "Look at May! Those two knights are bringing in May!" She was surrounded by a joyful crowd when she dismounted at the staircase; young men and squires ran up to hold her stirrup. More than a thousand knights from noble families hurried down from the balconies and from the upper floors of the marble palace. Everyone was amazed and struck dumb with wonder. She seemed a miracle or a beautiful enchantment, and many people said, "In times long ago, such maidens used to come bringing joy to the court of good King Arthur."

The knights ceremoniously led her into the palace; I don't think she had ever seen so many fine-looking people assembled in one place. Everyone gathered close to where the knights had seated her. This great assembly reminded her of her dear brother, since the emperor had convoked it because of his esteem for Guillaume's prowess and daring. And for love of Guillaume he had wanted Liénor to be his wife. At the thought of him her eyes filled with hot tears. She bowed her head and from time to time she sighed. The mighty lord of Speyer and many others felt pity for her. More than a hundred wept in sympathy. The tears that were falling from her eyes only made her more beautiful.

The singers and their songs could not cheer her up; she heard them begin to sing a song from Auvergne. If it weren't for the seneschal—may God punish him—who wanted to dishonor her, she could have sung it too.

> I delight to hear the lofty voice
> of the springtime nightingale,
> when leaves are green, flowers open white,
> grass is new on hill and dale,
> and the orchard trees are bright.
> If only my love could prevail,
> my body too would rejoice.[86]

The king, in the other room, was nearly out of his mind. Nothing that anyone said, did, or sang was any comfort to him. He heard the assembled barons speaking Flemish, but did not dare utter one word to them of what he had planned to say. The man who had caused him such misery was hardly a friend. They were all waiting for him to say something to them, or else ask the seneschal, his mortal enemy, to speak. While he sat under a great vaulted archway, utterly discouraged, the lord of Nivelles brought him the news: "Sire," he said, "haven't you heard what's happening outside? Not since the hour of Our Lord's birth, not even in the time of King Arthur, has such an amazing thing happened. Perhaps it's a sign of your luck!"

"What are you talking about?"

"A miracle of beauty has just arrived. I don't know whether she's a woman or a fairy, but there isn't a soul left in the marketplace. Everyone has accompanied her in a procession from a house in town right up to the palace."

The emperor, when he heard this, wouldn't have been happier if someone had given him a thousand marks. "I don't know whether he's telling the truth or joking," the seneschal said, "but it will be interesting to find out. Let's go and see." Now that evil demon is riding for a fall!

Said the king from his place at the entrance, "I agree with you." He needed no other excuse to postpone the assembly. He got up from where he was sitting and headed quickly for the palace, with all the barons following close behind.

Sad and tearful as she was (as much for her brother as for herself), the noble maiden, who was neither hunchbacked nor deformed, immediately recognized the emperor when he came out of his rooms where the meeting was held. According to custom, she unfastened the cord of her cloak. As she pulled it from her neck, it caught in the folds of her wimple so that helmet and coif and hood all came off. The knights saw her golden blond hair shining against her white skin and the indigo silk. Not since the days of Saint Paul had there been a woman whose beauty gave such pleasure. She was so little concerned with her own appearance that she hadn't even bothered to braid her hair; she had only combed it that morning, making a part with a porcupine quill, and it looked like a shining gold helmet.[87] She was wearing a chaplet in the fashion of the maidens of her region and her lovely locks curled about her face. The chaplet, set rather far back, was very becoming, and Nature had caused it to slip even further from her eyes in order to show off her beautiful forehead.

So, disarrayed and scarcely knowing what she was doing, she fell at the feet of the king and cried out: "For God's sake, help me!"

"Fair maiden!" the emperor said, "Get up or I'll die!"

"No! Right or wrong, I'll stay here all day unless you swear on the honor of your crown to grant me justice without the slightest delay."

"I swear it! There is nothing you could ask for that I would refuse." Then he stretched out his fine strong arms, and helped her to get up. She drew away from him a bit, with a becoming reserve.

Before all the knights of the realm, she made her lament, calling on God. Many wept for pity, seeing the tears running down her beautiful face, so lovely and so pure, and her neck, whiter than snow. I can tell you this, if she had been studying law for a full five years, she couldn't have stated her case more persuasively. The noble and gracious lady said, "Sire, my lord emperor, hear my plea, and may God help me in my need! One day, not long ago, that man over there, your seneschal (and she pointed at him), came into a room where I was sewing. What he did was hateful and cruel;

he robbed me of my virginity. After committing that vile crime, he stole my belt, my purse, and my brooch. I am here to demand restitution for my lost honor, my virginity, and my jewels."

Then she was silent. The emperor, who was greatly attracted to her, looked at the seneschal. The latter was completely unimpressed, considering it all a lie, just something she had dreamed up. (No one knew this better than Liénor!) The emperor said, "Seneschal, you have two choices. Either get some advice, or answer her accusations here and now. I am very much surprised to hear such a statement made about you."

The seneschal, in the presence of all the nobles of the empire, replied, "I don't need any advice! May God strike me dead if I've ever seen her before! I deny everything—I never took her virginity, nor did I steal her jewels, her belt, or her brooch."

"You have heard the seneschal," said the emperor. "He denies your accusations."

"Indeed, Sire, he is a very wicked man. He should have responded quite differently. If yours is a true court of justice, he won't leave this room a free man. Good king, I beg your pardon, but you say he denies it, that he never took my virginity or my brooch or my belt. Let me describe the belt to you. It was embroidered with a design of fish and birds worked in gold thread. The brooch was extremely valuable; it had a bright red ruby worth at least thirteen pounds. My accusation still stands. Look under his clothes and you'll see the belt against his bare flesh. If this isn't true you can have me run over by the wheels of a wagon! And you'll see the purse still hanging from the belt."

I think the seneschal is going to need some help! The color drained from his face; her words were all too true. "God!" said the knights assembled there, "if this really happened, he's in trouble. It's a very serious crime if she can prove it."

"Sire, you have promised me justice. Have the seneschal searched and pronounce your sentence right now."

The archbishop of Cologne, who happened to be present, said, "It has been a long time since such an accusation has been heard in your court, Sire. You should determine the truth of it without delay."

Without waiting for the seneschal to say yes or no, and whether he liked it or not, a knight took hold of him and pulled up his tunic and shirt. Everyone could see that he was wearing the belt tightly fastened around his bare body. There was obviously no need for further proof. "Guard him with your life!" said the emperor. "Make sure he doesn't get away!" He handed him over to ten venerable noblemen, ordering them, by all they held dear, to keep him in their custody. "I am greatly saddened by this," said the king, "for he has served me well."

"Ah!" say the seneschal's friends, "God willing, that will help him in his hour of need."

There's no use prolonging the story with idle words. Everyone was greatly troubled by the belt. Some said, "You can easily find belts like that. On such flimsy evidence he could hardly be put to death. The jewels and other things could be restored easily, but it's true that her virginity and her shame are quite another matter."

One by one, the lords came before the emperor to plead on the seneschal's behalf. "I will do anything you wish," replied the king, "as long as the maiden's honor is upheld."

"Such an accusation should not mean his death!"

To this the king responded, "There's no point in arguing. I wouldn't take a thousand gold marks to keep him from being dragged through the streets by horses or burned alive! Is my land devoid of honor? Being my seneschal didn't give him the right to steal such jewels!"

The maiden thanked him; what he had said convinced her that justice would be done. The seneschal's friends went back and told him he needed to get some advice. He angrily replied, "To hell with a court where an honest man's word is not enough![88] If the king wanted me to, I could get a hundred knights to swear that all my misfortune was caused by magic. How can I know for certain that this is her belt! But for God's sake! Conrad should remember our childhood, the service I've done him, our long friendship! He should at least do me the honor of believing me when I say that I've never seen her before, nor did I seek her dishonor or shame, nor did I take her virginity. After all I've done for the emperor, the least he can do is grant me a trial by ordeal. If I'm guilty, he can have me hanged on the spot! Give him this message for me."

His friends and the members of his household loudly lamented his fate: "What a sad day for us!" they said among themselves. "What are we going to do? We might as well be dead, since none of us can defend him. He was always so generous with his squirrel and miniver furs, and his great wealth; the horses he gave us were worth a fortune! Now he's going to be dragged through the streets or burned alive for something he didn't do."

I've never known a man to inspire such distress. The maiden herself was overcome with grief, believing that in accusing him she had committed a great sin. The noble lords went back to the emperor. On their knees, with tears streaming down their faces, they presented the seneschal's request.

The others said, "In the name of God, may the emperor do as they ask." Everyone respected Conrad's authority and his rights, but nothing like this had ever happened before.[89]

Tears of pity filled the emperor's eyes, for the seneschal had served him tirelessly and well. "My lords," he said, "I promise you I would rather have gone barefoot on a pilgrimage overseas than seen this happen."

In a few words the noblemen told him why they had come. She had made the belt appear on the seneschal by magic, they said, and it was of such a common design it would be easy to find one like it. "You could hardly want to see the man destroyed for something like this. So we're asking you to accept the statement he made: that until today he had never set eyes on her and that he never touched her naked flesh; she came to no harm through him. A trial by ordeal would establish the truth. He asks this of you as a reward for his service, and we ask that you grant it."

"I wouldn't do it for anyone, unless the maiden herself asked me to."

They threw themselves at her feet, imploring her to agree, for God's sake and their own; she would earn their hearts and eternal gratitude. They raised their clasped hands to her: "Ah! lady, it's a sin to destroy the vanquished!"

They begged and pleaded so much that at last she agreed. She asked God to perform a miracle clearly demonstrating that she did not deserve the loss she had suffered. Everyone there said, "Amen!" The emperor and all his retinue were overjoyed that she had consented.

The ordeal took place immediately at an ivy-covered church called Saint Peter's. All the princes and other highborn nobles came; and, following the advice of the archbishops, the maiden also was present to ensure that justice be done. When the seneschal appeared, many looked at him with contempt because of the belt. Straight down, as soon as he entered the holy water, straight down, faster than a woodsman's axe, he sank to the bottom. The fair Liénor, and all the others grouped around the basin, saw that he was proven innocent. The priests praised God, singing; bells were rung.

Amidst great celebration, the seneschal was brought before the emperor, who was absolutely delighted. All the others were, too. The maiden immediately returned to the palace. Things had turned out exactly as she had planned. She went directly to the emperor who was rejoicing over the great honor God had shown to his seneschal. She was indifferent to the happiness around her; there was great sorrow in her heart because of her beloved brother. "Maiden," the emperor said, "the seneschal has been acquitted."

"He whose praises the priests sing in church," said the noble Liénor, "well knows how to answer prayers and help those of good will. Ask your people to listen to me now. For God's sake, Sire, hear me out! I am the maiden of the rose, the sister of my lord Guillaume, who by his prowess had won for me the honor of your kingdom."

So great was her distress that tears streamed down her face. "This man (may I see him torn to pieces!) made a trip to our home, pretending to be our friend. My mother, who believed him, told him about the rose I have on my thigh. Dear God in heaven, let me make my case! Not a soul knew about it, except my brother, my mother and myself. I could die of shame from telling you all this!"

"Dear God!" said the counts, many of whom were shocked by this news. "How could anyone behave so treacherously?"

"This man is a proven traitor; he hates my family, and that's why he told you the outrageous lie that I was not a virgin. God who was born of Mary has proven my innocence, and unless your court fails me, my honor will be restored before I leave. I should have won my case as soon as he was found in possession of my belt, even though he had denied it. Had justice been done, he would already have been hanged as a criminal. But the nobles, who pitied him, prevailed on you to reopen the trial in order to examine his denial, his statement that he had never seen me before that day or done anything to cause me shame. That was the truth, so help me God! You have all seen how we were both exonerated by his ordeal; he did not have my virginity nor did he dishonor me. If I am destined to rule this kingdom, why should this unhappy creature be denied an honor she has done nothing to lose? This is what I would ask the justice of the court."

Then the emperor said, "Is it really you, my beloved?"

She replied, "I am fair Liénor."

He jumped up and everyone saw him put his fine strong arms around her and kiss her lovely eyes and her face over and over again. Said he: "Be happy, for God has done you great honor!" Because of the tremendous joy he felt, this song sprang from his heart:

> "What more do you want,
>   when I am yours?
> What more do you want—
>   am I not yours?"
> "Just this will do,
>   if you love me true."

And the others all sang:

> Hold out your hands for the summer flowers,
>   the lily flowers,
> Oh, hold out your hands!

That was their *Te Deum laudamus*.

The emperor said: "Now you know the reason for this great assembly today. I have long been aware that you are unhappy because I have no wife; you have been concerned about the succession—that it might fall into the hands of another king who might not honor and serve you as I do. And that could have happened. The lessons of childhood are easiest to follow. My desire to serve you has never been greater—I swear it by my hope that God will protect me, body and soul, in my hour of greatest need."

Anyone who didn't shed tears on hearing him pronounce those words was hard-hearted indeed. "Fame, which travels far and wide, brought this maiden to my attention. And she is the one for whom I intend this honor if, for my sake and out of your love for me, you accept her as the lady and queen of my realm. You are my knights and my noble lords; therefore, if, rightly or wrongly, you do not agree to it, this marriage will not take place, although it would still be my desire."

With these words he convinced them all, on the spot, to agree. Everyone who desired to please the emperor hastened to say: "I wish it." Further discussion and counsel were not needed; there was unanimous approbation.

Their good king, pious and kind, expressed his gratitude repeatedly. "Thank God!" he said, "now the noble Guillaume will be cured."

Some of them ran for their horses, to go tell the news to Liénor's brother! They found him, disconsolate, in his host's orchard. Though the nightingales were singing to him, they gave him no pleasure. But the good news, which was quickly told, took away all his sorrow. His people said: "All we have to do now is celebrate!"

Guillaume changed the fur-lined cloak on which he had shed so many tears for one made of samite, beautifully embroidered with his arms on the front and sleeves. It had been fashioned with great care and had never been worn; it was suitable for summer, the lining light as a feather.[90] How little it took to make him handsome once again! Astride his horse he rode in the midst of some hundred splendidly mounted knights, all eager to do him honor. They had not gone far when the bishop of Liège's charming nephew began to sing this song:

Now that April's beauty can be seen,
the woods in flower, meadows once more green,
the sweet waters moving through their streams,
and birds sing in the morning and at eve,
let those who love not love forgetfully,
but soon return again when they take leave.

. . . .

. . . .

In love are young Count Guy and fair Aigline.
Guy loves Aigline, Aigline loves young Guy.

At a noble castle—its name is Beauclaire—
a great ball has been swiftly prepared.
Girls take part in the dances there,
squires go to cast their lances there,
knights to watch out for their chances there,
ladies attract their glances there.
And to that castle comes Aigline; she wears
a tunic of the finest silk, whose train
extends across the meadow a long way.
Guy loves Aigline, Aigline loves young Guy.

This song had not been sung all the way through when a knight from the
region of Dammartin began to sing this Poitevin song:

When I see a lark on the wing,
rising in joy toward the light,
then lost in its rapture, falling,
its heart overcome by delight,
that vision of rejoicing
such envy in me inspires,
it seems I will go insane,
overwhelmed by my heart's desire.

Alas! I thought I knew so much
about love, but I was blind.
I cannot keep from loving
one who will always be unkind.
She has taken my heart, my being,
her own self, and the entire

world except what I retain:
my yearning and my heart's desire.[91]

When these two had finished, a nice young man remembered these lovely
verses by Gontier de Soignies and began to sing them:

When the heather blooms in spring,
and I see the meadows green,
and birds, in their own way, sing
from branches high in the trees,
my heart can only sigh
in its cruel suffering
from her answer to my pleas
and my long, useless, waiting.

I love her so,
and my heart is full of sorrow.
Alas! Love brings me woe
and a heart full of sorrow.

Unworthy it is, and madness
to love and yet not to fear.
True lovers conceal their prowess,
hide what they hold most dear.
Unworthy are lovers unless
there's no sign when they appear,
so that none feel joy or gladness
save the one whose love is near.

I love her so . . .

They proceeded to the court in very high spirits. The people along the
way said: "Look! Here comes the brother of the queen!"

And when he arrived at the palace they all said, "A better or handsomer
young man will never go in!"

"What a lucky day for me," said Guillaume, "when I see my sister so
honored by my lord that he has seated her beside him on the throne!" He
removed the cloak from around his neck and went to kneel before them.

"My sweet brother, my dear heart," said she, "you are welcome indeed!"

He could have wept at such a greeting. He answered her with respect, as his sovereign lady, and I want you to know that he touched her only with his words. This was appreciated by everyone who noticed. He had sense enough to realize that his sister's new dignity precluded familiarity and gestures of affection. He pushed his left arm into the laces of his cloak.[92] Henceforth he was lord and master of the court and its noble lords.

Said the emperor: "It is time that I spoke of my plans. Should I wait until the Feast of the Ascension for my wedding?"

"God willing," they replied, "there seems no reason at all for delay."

"Sire," said the Duke of Saxony, "by the hour of God's birth! Do what you need to do! If everyone goes home, it will be a nuisance to come back later. We're all here now."

Said the archbishop, "That sounds like good advice to me."

To which the emperor replied, "If all of you are willing, I agree."

Ah! Sex pulls harder than a rope! He never wanted anything so much!

"By God!" said the king, "now everything's fine, providing you all approve. Go and get ready, my lord," he said to the archbishop, who went off with at least ten bishops to dress at his residence.

When the townspeople learned that God had granted the maiden good fortune, there was excitement such as had not been seen since the sinless birth of God. They hastened to send her many ladies from all over the city; highborn wives of knights came most willingly to adorn and dress her. Not since Alexander made his famous leap at Tyre had there been such joy in people's hearts.[93]

A fairy had made the fabric of the empress's robes. It was tightly woven, and had been embroidered long ago by a queen of Puglia who had used her needle to pass the time agreeably in her chambers.[94] It took her at least seven or eight years to complete the work. On it was depicted the story of Helen's birth; Helen herself was there, along with Paris and his brother Hector, King Priam, and King Memnon, who did so many good deeds. The images showing Paris kidnapping Helen were of gold and also those of the Greeks coming to look for her. Achilles, who caused such grief by killing Hector, was also portrayed, and the burning of the city and how they hid in the wooden horse. It showed the Greek fleet being plundered while Achilles lay on carpets in his tent.[95] No one alive knows how to make such beautiful cloth. The lining was neither miniver nor gray squirrel; rather it was black sable and ermine overlapping, delicately scented. Anyone could be content even if he had nothing else to wear. Everyone praised its exquisite workmanship. But everyone prized the maiden's face and beauty far more.

With great joy the nobles now led her to the church. So much oriental silk and gold brocade, so much diapered fabric and samite had never been seen in one place, nor so many differently ornamented gowns, some with birds, others with fish, and yet others with four panels each of a different color. Cloaks were fully lined with whole pelts of fine sable.

The entire treasure of the church was brought forth in a procession. There was a famous reliquary, but of what origin I do not know; there was a scepter and, without going into all the details, everything needed for the coronation of an emperor. Conrad and Liénor each had a magnificent crown which the archbishop placed on their heads immediately after the wedding. Next, with suitable pomp, mass was celebrated in honor of the Holy Spirit, and there was singing in praise of the Trinity.

The servants had so hastened to do their various tasks that, as soon as everyone came from the church, cloths were spread on the tables. I don't know why I'm prolonging the story with idle words. But after the basins of water were brought around, those whose high birth had destined them for the honor were seated close to the empress: dukes and archbishops and other nobles and bishops. Those seated at the high tables[96] were astonished by her beauty. They said, "She could steal your heart away, but who would call it theft?"

Some spoke among themselves of the seneschal: "Now surely he must be ashamed of his treachery. He should be among those men of noble family whose right and duty it is to serve their lord when he wears his crown."

The vassals, according to their rank, served at table that day to honor the emperor in all his splendor.

"The seneschal has forfeited this privilege," said others, "and it's his own fault. He'll pay dearly for this; the emperor despises him now."[97]

The seneschal, with his legs in irons and manacles on his hands, was already in the tower. He would have to be as clever as Renard to escape.[98] A singer from Thouars, a member of the lord of Huy's household, was giving little thought to the seneschal's troubles, and neither did the many others who went about singing:

> Down there, down there in the meadow, they say,
> it's not for you to dance, my ladies.
> The fair Aelis will soon be at play
>   under the green olive tree;
> it's not for you to dance, my ladies,
>   where only lovers can go.

> But I am to dance, and there I'll be,
> for the lady I love loves me!

A count said, "I don't see anyone here with as much right to sing this song as my lord the emperor."

"True enough," he replied, "and this song too; it's better than most things to fill the space between courses."

> Down there in the meadow
> I have found my heart's desire.
> The dancing had begun
> when my eyes saw one—
> I have found my heart's desire.
> all I require.

Nothing more appropriate could be sung at this celebration in his honor and for his joy.

To count the dishes isn't easy, there were so many different ones: boar and bear and venison, cranes, wild geese, and roasted peacock. The servants did no dishonor to those to whom they brought a ragout of vegetables and lamb (which was in season, since it was May), and fat beef and force-fed goslings. Everyone had the choice of red and white wines. The emperor, replete, gazed at his great assembly of nobles and at the face of his newly-crowned wife. His people had welcomed her so warmly that he held them even more dear.

His brother-in-law certainly took great pleasure in this occasion. He was the most elegant knight you could possibly see when, wearing no cloak, he served the emperor at table. God! if their dear mother could have seen her children so honored, she would have had good health all the rest of her days! Those who went to bring her the news were told not to linger along the way!

After the tablecloths had been removed, the sons of noblemen brought towels and basins full of clear water. The emperor, having been so well served, washed his hands, as did the empress, the archbishop, and then the others. The festivities began and would continue all night long. They spent the rest of the day jousting and amusing themselves, and so much clothing and sumptuous finery was distributed that everyone who came in hopes of largesse was well satisfied. The nobles who desired Conrad's good will contributed so many traveling cloaks, tunics, doublets, and capes, that a comparable amount of white fabric could have clothed all the monks of Igny and Ourscamps for three years.[99] So there was a great abundance to give away.

But I haven't begun to tell you about the king's happiness that night. His were all the joys that a man can have when he holds his beloved close to him in bed. If you took Tristan at the time when he most loved Iseut, and could hold her and kiss her and do everything else he desired, and Lanval and twenty other famous lovers I could name, all their happiness put together could not be compared to Conrad's. That was apparent the next morning, when no one who asked him for a costly gift was refused.

Before the emperor left and the noble lords dispersed, an abundance of beautiful things were presented to them according to their service and their rank. With one voice they asked mercy for the seneschal.

"I am saddened by your pleas, but even for as much gold as there is brass in Huy, where they make cauldrons, I would not forsake justice." The Duke of Savoy and the others, in great distress, prostrated themselves on the alabaster floor. "It's no use. Get up now. There is nothing more in this world for that traitor who lied to me and tried to dishonor a noble lady. Out of envy he almost destroyed the worthiest of women. Surely he must hate himself, for he will die in shame."

"Since this concerns my lady, dear Sire, would it displease you if we spoke to her about it?"

"Not at all; let it be just as she wishes." He regretted having refused them so quickly, for they had served him well and with great generosity. They were wise to think of the queen, and went to her right away. One spoke for them all; if the seneschal died or was maimed, she would gain little, but if she agreed to do what they asked, she would win their hearts forever.

Liénor was beautifully dressed, adorned and coiffed. The emperor—thank God—had not caused her such suffering during the night that she couldn't respond as she should, without vindictiveness, and without neglecting a single word of what they said to her.[100] They made sure she realized that the emperor would allow her to do as she desired.

"I could indeed be harsh with him, if my lord has truly left this up to me. But I do not want God and the German people to have any cause for complaint; that would not be right. Now give me your advice. Can there be a fair penalty in this case other than death or maiming? Lest anyone be inspired to follow his example, I don't want him to get out of this without doing a lengthy penance."

"Make him leave France and Germany and go overseas."

"I shouldn't be too easy on him, since he certainly doesn't deserve it. Let him serve with the Templars, if my husband will agree."

"Yes, lady, I promise he will."

"Then that is what I desire, for the love of God and for you."

"Lady, from God and from all of us, grateful thanks! Your kindness has taken a great weight off our minds."

They then went to tell the emperor what she had said. He replied, "By the Holy Spirit, I will not countermand it. By imposing so slight a penance for so outrageous a crime, she does not return evil for evil."

"Sire, now everything will be as it should be. We should put this behind us, and never think of it again. There has been shame and grief enough."

"May God, by whose grace we are so happy, give the seneschal a good day today. Go quickly and have his shackles removed. But the fellow had better be sure he's wearing the clothes of a crusader when he comes back to my court. He'll have my love again when Hell freezes over!"[101]

Dressed as a crusader, the seneschal was brought in, weeping, to express his gratitude and thanks to the empress for the goodness she had shown him. Yet I can tell you that he was far from happy, having never thought he'd be exiled from the court. Afterwards, the nobles wished to take their leave of the empress. She granted it to them most graciously, with brief and charming words, and the emperor did the same. Then they left the court and returned to their own lands where each had much to do. It is indeed an ill-natured world where all joy ends up doleful. They would never have wanted to leave, but they had to. The emperor and twenty knights remained with the empress. Her brother Guillaume was a beloved and powerful lord. It gave the emperor much pleasure to see their mother when she came, and he saw to her needs most handsomely there in Mainz.

It was the archbishop who had the story written down to honor them all. Kings and counts should certainly remember the worthy man whose story has been told, and try to do as much good as he did all his life long.[102] His praises will be sung as long as the world endures, which will be for some time yet.

And now he wishes to rest, this one who lost his surname on the day he eNTeRed on A REligious life.[103]

Here ends The Romance of the Rose.

Notes

1. Although the one extant manuscript of *Guillaume de Dole* has only the texts of the songs without music, the prologue contains the verb *noter*, which can refer to musical notation.

2. Anthime Fourrier suggests that in heraldry the first color mentioned is that of the field rather than of the figure (p. 1212). Along with Dufournet we follow Fourrier's emendation of this passage.

3. King Mark was the husband of Iseut in the story of *Tristan and Iseut*.

4. The ladies' white gloves represent not only the elegance of their attire but also the general context of idleness and ease. Cf. the depiction of Oiseuse in Guillaume de Lorris's *Romance of the Rose*:

> . . . por garder que ses mains blanches
> Ne halassent ot uns blans gans. (ll. 562–63)
> (. . . to prevent her white hands
> from being sunburned, she wore white gloves.)

5. The text reads, "Ça, chevalier, as dames!" (l. 223; literally, "To the ladies, knights!"). This is Jean Renart's variation on the battle cry, "To arms, knights!" The expression also occurs in certain manuscripts of *Le Lai de l'Ombre*.

6. See Appendix 1 on Clothing.

7. For a list of first lines of poems and known authors, see Appendix 2.

8.   que chascuns i garist et sane
       ses oils d'esgarder les mervelles (ll. 359–60)

Literally, "for each one healed his eyes by looking at [these] marvels."

9. Constant is the name of a farmer in the *Roman de Renart*. Renard the fox attempts to steal his prize rooster, Chantecler.

10. Lejeune tells us that Eudes de Ronquerolles was well known during the reign of Philip Augustus; Jean Renart's reference to him here suggests an ironic comparison (*Oeuvres*, pp. 90–91).

11. "Dehez ait sanz moi qui t'aprist!" (l. 648). We follow here Lecoy's gloss of *sanz moi* as "moi excepté" (1961, p. 244).

12.   "La biauté, le pris del Barrois
        au jor que plus en pot avoir,
        ce sachiez de fi et de voir,
        si fu noienz avers cestui." (ll. 671–74)

According to Lejeune, Guillaume II des Barres was indeed greatly admired for his valor as well as his beauty. He was one of the most famous and faithful knights of Philip Augustus (*Oeuvres*, pp. 92–93).

13. Since Jouglet's description is totally conventional, the author's praise may be ironic. That Jouglet had always intended that his abstract portrait be eclipsed by the "real" lady from Dole is indicated by his choice of "Dol" in l. 715. Dol is located in present-day Brittany. Dole is southeast of Dijon.

14. It is now generally agreed that Jouglet's story refers to *Le Lai de l'Ombre*. His description of the heroine, while conventional, corresponds to subsequent descriptions of Liénor. There is no detailed portrait of the lady in *Le Lai de l'Ombre*.

15. The play on the words *cuer* (heart) and *cor* (body) could not be reproduced in the translation.

16. The "story" is never finished for the very good reason that Jean Renart had already written it.

17. Since the emperor has never met Guillaume, this comment would seem to be a reference to a public appearance by Conrad.

18. It is not at all clear what these instructions mean, nor does it seem likely that the horse would be identified without explanation as belonging to, or having belonged to, the Count of Perche. One wonders whether the horse is being designated by its type. The "great horse," which could accommodate an armored knight, was first developed in the geographical setting of *Guillaume de Dole*, including Perche, whose horses would later be known as Percherons.

19.   "—Ja ne voudrez que je n'en face:
par cest covent dirai encore" (ll. 1198–99)

Our translation of this difficult line follows Lecoy's interpretation (1961, pp. 249–52), also cited by Dufournet.

20.   "Or avez le gré et l'amor
et la querele et voz amis." (ll. 1222–23)

The exact meaning of *querele* (our "thanks") in this context cannot be determined.

21. "Il vous guile." Another example of the play on Guillaume's name.

22.   s'ist de la vile entor plessiee (l. 1287).
Plessiée here refers to the protective hedge surrounding the village. It is later used in the text as a synonym for Guillaume's home.

23. Blood-letting was practiced from early times with the idea that excess of blood was a cause of disease. Danielle Régnier-Bohler has observed that in the literature of the Middle Ages "bleeding marked the beginning of a withdrawal into a private realm, not always without elements of parody." In *Erec et Enide* Arthur is bled with some five hundred knights present, but complains that "he was bored not to have more of his court with him" (p. 366).

24.   Cel jor fesoit chanter la suer
a un jougleor mout apert
qui chante cest vers de Gerbert (ll. 1332–34)

The passage may be read either as "he had the sister of a very clever minstrel sing," or as "the sister had a very clever minstrel sing."

In l. 1368 (immediately following the song), we are told that *"cil* chante de Fromont," which indicates that the singer is male. This confusion may be the result of a scribal error.

25. "Me fet pas a son beau non honte" (l. 1421). Literally, "She does not bring shame to her beautiful name." Conrad's comment is based on the word play *bele Lïenors* and *com li ors* (like gold).

26. This description of Guillaume is drawn from the portrait of King Memnon in the *Roman de Troie*.

27. Lejeune suggests that the reference is ironic, pointing to a man known for his lack of elegance (*Oeuvres*, p. 146).

28. ". . . devant l'Endit" (l. 1600). Lejeune notes that this fair took place on the second Wednesday in June (*GD*, p. 180). Since this is at most six weeks away, Conrad's enthusiasm is more restrained than might at first appear.

29. On references to Troy, see Introduction, p. 8.

30.   Il li a demandé s'il ere
           point privez dou roi d'Engleterre. (ll. 1626–27)

Lejeune has commented on the awkwardness of this passage. While we agree with her reading (i.e., it is Conrad who asks Guillaume the question about the King of England), we do not interpret the passage in quite the same way. There seems little support for her claim that "The author is making fun of this first meeting" (*GD*, p. 146).

31. *com las bués marge* (l. 1643) can also mean, how to tell an ox's condition from the way it is moving, or, what makes an ox move more quickly; figuratively, how to get things done.

32. Saint-Trond, Old French *Sainteron*, is the modern French form of Saint Truiden in Belgium.

33. We have slightly altered Lecoy's punctuation here. The following line seems to us a comment by the narrator, rather than a continuation of Guillaume's remark.

34. The French term used is *fabliaus*.

35.   mout vient a home de grant sen,
           qui fet cortoisie au besoig. (ll. 2064–65)

These lines also occur in *Le Lai de l'Ombre* (ll. 914–15). Jean Renart makes the shrewd observation that courtly behavior often brings tangible rewards.

36.   Maint vilain i ot mesmarchié,
           qui musoient a Constantin. (ll. 2074–75)

The exact meaning of *muser a Constantin* is not known.

37.   vos n'esloignerez vos sergenz
           por tornoier demie lance! (ll. 2116–17)

Lecoy interprets the line as follows: "you will not succeed in leaving your camp [more than] the length of a half lance, no matter how much enthusiasm you bring to the fighting" (p. 181). Our reading is closer to that of Dufournet.

38. *come borjois* (l. 2175), literally, like one of the town's more comfortable inhabitants.

39. *car prodom a en poi assez* (l. 2190). Since Guillaume is clearly concerned with the appearance of wealth (to the extent that he borrows an impressive surname), this comment would seem to be an ironic aside on the part of the narrator.

40. We have adopted Lecoy's reading (1961, pp. 232–53).

41. *Un pasté de .ii. paons manz* (l. 2216). Lecoy proposes *châtré* (castrated), but notes that the term is unique. We suppose that gelding makes birds fatter.

42. The lines so indicated are either missing or illegible in the unique extant copy of the manuscript.

43. Vivien is an important figure in the French epic *Guillaume d'Orange*.

44. Saint George is the patron saint of knights.

45. Lejeune observes: "Jean Renart wants to oppose French politeness to the German lack of gallantry" (*Oeuvres*, p. 152).

46.   "A! Dex!, fet l'une, qui est cil
           a la cote de mustadole?" (ll. 2538–39)

Although the meaning of *mustadole* is unknown, it seems clearly to refer to fabric. The term incorporates Guillaume's adopted surname.

47. A fictional hero.

48. "Something extraordinary" translates *aventure*, the word used for the marvelous experiences of King Arthur's knights. Its use here would be mildly ironic. In ll. 4617–19 and 4681–83, Liénor's arrival at court is specifically compared to Arthurian *aventures*, and here the comparison is all in favor of Liénor.

49. Part of this sentence is missing in the manuscript; the reference, however, is clearly to Guillaume.

50.   Fet Juglés: "Dole! chevalier!
           C'est Guillames Aporte bos!" (ll. 2666–67)

Lecoy comments that "Aporte bos" (bring wood) is a compliment; Guillaume is using a great number of lances (1979, p. 181).

51. This refers to the supplier from Liège who had sent equipment to Guillaume on credit.

52. Michel de Harnes was the leader of the French side, and, like all the other named participants in the tournament, a historical figure. Lejeune says that he was "One of the rare Flemish and Artesian noblemen to show exemplary faithfulness to Philip Augustus" (*Oeuvres*, pp. 106–7).

53. We have followed Lecoy's emendation of *resoignent* (they fear) to *repoignent* (they spur) (p. 225).

54. Early Israelite heroes (2nd century BC), who successfully resisted the Syrians.

55. We follow Dufournet's reading of *harnués* as "camp" (p. 59).

56. Another interpretation of this line would be that the members of Conrad's household had spoken favorably of Guillaume.

57.   Et por ce ne l'osa nomer
           por doutance de l'aperçoivre. (ll. 3002–3)

We have followed Dufournet's reading of this line. Jouglet had already told Conrad Liénor's name, which was "a spark Love kindled in his breast."

58. Lienor's status as an *orfenine* (l. 3043) refers to the death of her father.

59. King Arthur's seneschal Kay was well known for his bad temper and jealousy of other knights.

60. The song is anonymous. One wonders whether Jean Renart himself composed it for the occasion. In any case, the emperor is not only a singer of songs but here, at least, said to be a poet.

61.　　　La dame a a son col geté
　　　un grant mantel gris a porfil,
　　　dont l'atache n'est pas de fil,
　　　mes l'escarlate en est en paine. (ll. 3280–83)

We follow Lejeune's reading, except for her interpretation of *paine* (lining) as a form of *peine* (pain), although we have no alternative explanation.

62.　　　Il est toz sires et toz mestre
　　　de mon segnor, tant a vescu. (ll. 3322–23)

The meaning of the expression *tant a vescu* remains uncertain.

63.　　　Un petitet, un mervelleus,
　　　en avoient si chamberlenc,
　　　et s'ert plus tendres d'un herenc,
　　　si l'apeloit on Cupelin. (ll. 3398–3401)

The exact meaning of the phrase "plus tendres d'un herenc" (more tender than a herring) is unknown. Dufournet translates the phrase "aussi fluet qu'un hareng" (as supple and quick as a herring) with the note that "tendre" may be an ironic "antiphrase," meaning "dry" or "hard." Lejeune (*GD*, p. 157; *Oeuvres*, pp. 168–69), discusses the unusual nature of the comparison, and concludes that "tendre" means "petit et fluet."

64.　　　Cest vers de bele Marguerite,
　　　qui si bel se paie et aquite
　　　de la chançonete novele,
　　　li fet chanter en la vïele (ll. 3415–18)

Line 3415 is ambiguous. Is Marguerite the composer of the song, or is the song about her? Along with Dufournet we follow the second interpretation.

65.　　　Fet chascuns: "Ceste i vet mout bien.
　　　—Celes ne l'en doivent de rien,
　　　fet li rois, se le volez dire." (ll. 3431–33)

Again, a difficult passage. We follow Lecoy's suggestion that *ceste* (this one) refers to Marguerite and that Conrad's reference to *celes* (these) is to the ladies of his entourage whom he invites the others to admire (p. 183).

66.　　　Onc puis le tenz Robert Macié
　　　tele traïson ne fu fete. (ll. 3458–59)

No reference to a historical figure named Robert Macié has been found.

67.   por passer les chievres, les chous,
                    sachiez qu'il n'estoit mie fous. (ll. 3471–72)

A reference to a proverbial dilemma: how can a wolf, a goat, and a cabbage cross a river together? (See Lecoy, p. 204.)

68. We have not followed Lecoy's punctuation, according to which this phrase (ll. 3477–78) is spoken by Conrad in response to the seneschal. The comment resembles other asides by the narrator.

69. Islande (l. 3531). As Lecoy notes, probably a scribal "lapsus" for "Irlande" (p. 192).

70. Saint Julian was the patron saint of travelers.

71. Guillaume's statement here raises a question about his gift of the emperor's seal to Liénor in ll. 1002–3: *Sa suer, la bele Liénors, / en ot l'or por un soen fermail*. The passage suggests that Liénor will make a brooch out of the seal; it might, however, be argued that Liénor gives Guillaume a brooch *in exchange for* the seal.

72. *herbe pestre* (to eat grass) was a common expression meaning to be insane. It derives from the story of King Nebuchadnezzar, punished by God for his pride (*Daniel* 4. 28–37).

73.   "Ahi! font ses genz d'Alemaigne,
                    de quex genz estes dessamblee?" (ll. 3782–83)

We have adopted Le Gentil's suggestion that l. 3782 refers to the Germans (cited by Dufournet, p. 77).

74. *Uns siens niés* (l. 3786). Probably a reference to a young cousin. Liénor is later referred to as his cousin (l. 3946). The term did not have its present specificity in the twelfth and thirteenth centuries.

75. Guillaume's reaction seems singularly egocentric. It underscores the role of women in the formation of advantageous family alliances.

76.   Un jor li sovint de la bele
                    qui porte le sornon de Dole,
                    que il looit tant par parole;
                    onqes ne la virent si oeil. (ll. 3874–77)

We prefer Servois's reading, *l'ooit* ("heard," l. 3866) to Lecoy's *looit* ("praised," l. 3876). Conrad's sudden recollection indicates that Guillaume has temporarily taken Liénor's place in his affections.

77.   Li vallez voit qu'il ne puet rien
                    gaaignier en fere mellee,
                    si ra mis el fuerre s'espee,
                    qu'il a grant pitié de s'aiole,
                    qui sa mere bese et acole. (ll. 3998–4002)

As Lecoy notes, *aiole* is evidently a reference to the mother; it is therefore necessary to emend *mere* to *fille* in l. 4002 (p. 183).

78. Liénor's comment suggests that the mother has told her all about her talk with the seneschal.

79. The term used is *vavassors*; gentlemen from the lower nobility with (as Lecoy notes) "modest income."

80. . . . *en romanz sanz latin* (l. 4195)—that is, to speak in the vernacular, or directly.

81.   "Une pucele le me dit
       qui en porta mout les messages." (ll. 4325–26)

Liénor's claim may or may not be true. There is a lively mix of fact and fiction in this passage, and perhaps an allusion to the messenger maidens of Arthurian tradition.

82. *robë* in line 4350 probably refers to the complete costume, as in ll. 4445–46, but it is unclear of what the costume consisted. Dufournet (p. 88) agrees with Lejeune that "la cote en puret" means that Liénor wore only a tunic when she went to court. But, as Goddard points out, the cloak was "an integral part of the costume of a person of rank, essential to a complete toilet" (p. 163). Liénor first puts on the tunic of green silk, and then the indigo samite cloak. When she arrives at court, she starts to untie her cloak, but it catches in her headdress. Then her golden hair is seen against an indigo fabric.

83. Liénor is here compared to two women of the French epic tradition: Bertha, the mother of Charlemagne, and Olivier's sister Aude, Roland's betrothed in *The Song of Roland*, who dies instantly on learning of Roland's death.

84. The meaning of the term *acor* (l. 4514) is not altogether clear; we have followed Lecoy's definition (p. 198).

85. Following Lejeune's reading of *place du change*.

86. We adopt Servois's edition for the last two lines.

87. The description of Liénor includes a number of references to protective headgear worn as part of armor. We assume that her headdress is only figuratively a helmet; she has come to court to fight for her honor and is therefore dressed for battle. The expression *si ot fet front de heaumiere* (l. 4735), literally, "made her look like a helmet maker," may refer to a particular hair style.

88.   "Mal de la cort ou l'en ne let,
       fet il, un home parjurer!" (ll. 4906–7)

Lecoy notes that *parjurer* has only one attested meaning in Old French: *faire un faux serment* (to swear a false oath). He proposes adopting Servois's reading of the line as "se justifier par serment" (to justify oneself by an oath). However, there may have been a scribal error (1961, pp. 256–60).

89. We have slightly altered Lecoy's punctuation. Lines 4948–51 do not seem to be part of the "others'" response to the seneschal's request.

90.   Mout fu legiere por esté,
       que la pene en estoit d'oiseaus. (ll. 5177–78)

Literally, "it was light for summer, for the lining was made out of *oiseaus*." The last word could mean either that the lining was made of bird feathers, as Dufournet would have it, or else, that the cloak was unlined, Lecoy's interpretation. In this instance, however, the expression seems to be figurative.

91. Line 6 has been completed with reference to the Provençal text cited by Lecoy.

92.   El a bouté par mi les laz
de son mantel son braz senestre. (ll. 5280–81).

Guillaume's gesture is not readily identifiable, although it seems to reflect his elegance and discretion. No doubt the minstrel who performed this text orally would have imitated Guillaume's gesture, making it clear to the audience.

The use of *el* (she) poses a problem. Servois emended it to *il* (he). The action described could possibly have been an affectionate gesture from Liénor.

93. Alexander the Great laid siege to the Phoenician city of Tyre in 332 BC; after seven months he managed to scale its walls and enter the city, where he slaughtered some 10,000 of its inhabitants. Jean Renart would have read a fictional account of Alexander's "leap" in *Le Roman d'Alexandre*, which appeared toward the end of the twelfth century. Since he refers to the conquest of Tyre in *L'Escoufle* (ll. 8058–59) as an occasion of the greatest imaginable suffering, one wonders whether the joy referred to in *Guillaume de Dole* is that of the invaders. The allusion is, perhaps, intended to be ironic.

94.   D'un drap quë une fee ouvra
fu vestue l'empereriz;
il n'iert ne tiessuz ne tresliz,
ainçois l'ot tot fet o agulle
jadis une roïne en Puille,
en ses chambres por son deduit. (ll. 5324–29)

This is an obscure passage, since both the fairy and the queen seem to have manufactured the material for Liénor's dress. We suggest that the references to weaving (*tiessuz*, woven; *tresliz*, loosely woven) indicate that the fairy made the exceptional fabric, which was then suitable for a queen's embroidery. As this is the only fairy in this work, we might point out that four fairies embroidered the quadrivium on Erec's coronation robe in Chrétien de Troyes's *Erec et Enide*.

95. Along with Dufournet, we understand the *tapis* (carpets) to refer to those on which Achilles reclined in his tent.

96. A distinction is made in the passage between the two kinds of tables: the *dois* (l. 5389), on which cloths were spread, are tables set up on trestles that could be disassembled after use. The *tables dormanz* (l. 5397) at which the nobles and high officials are seated are permanent tables.

97. "car il le tient pires q'escoufles" (l. 5417); literally, the emperor "considers him worse than a kite," or bird of prey. *L'Escoufle* is the title of Jean Renart's earlier romance.

98.   S'il puet eschaper a cest tor,
dont savra il mout de Renart. (ll. 5420–21)

This reference to the protagonist of *Le Roman de Renart* suggests a play on Jean Renart's name, or perhaps he had taken that of the fox so renowned for his cleverness. He does, of course, contrive that the seneschal escape.

99. *blans buriaus* (l. 5497) is white fustian. Igny and Ourscamps were the sites of Cistercian abbeys. Cistercian monks wore only white garb.

100. This description of Liénor's wedding night is intriguing. It would seem that Conrad's gentleness made her particularly well disposed toward her petitioners.

101.   *"c'iert en l'eure que li chiens cort*
           qu'il i sera ja mes amez!"* (ll. 5615–16; our emphasis)

The meaning of this expression is not known. Lejeune observes that Servois "thought that *chieus* was altered; that in reality it was *ciu*, relating to blindness." The meaning would therefore be, " 'it's when the blind man runs that the seneschal will be tolerated,' which is to say never. *Chieus* is a Picard form" (*GD*, p. 173; also quoted by Dufournet). Lecoy's reading of the term is *chiens* (dog).

102. It has generally been assumed that the *prodome* (worthy man) is Conrad. However, the phrase *por avoir de bien fere envie* (l. 5648) recalls an earlier description of King Memnon, whose portrait in the *Roman de Troie* is used verbatim to describe Guillaume. In the description of Liénor's wedding cloak, Memnon is said to be *li bons rois qui toz les biens fist* (l. 5337). Memnon's exact contribution to society is not known.

103.   Et cil se veut reposer ore,
           qui le jor perdi son sornon
           qu'il enTRA EN Religion. (ll. 5653–55)

This acrostic for RENART was discovered by Joseph Bédier and is discussed in Lecoy's introduction to his edition of *Le Lai de l'Ombre*, p. xi. Our capitalization of the name is, however, a departure from Lecoy's text.

Appendix 1: Clothing in the Thirteenth Century

Modern readers of *Guillaume de Dole* not only confuse the names of real and fictional people, they are also unlikely to notice its display of the latest fashions in dress, styles transitional from those of the twelfth century, less ornate but no less elegant. The most distinctive twelfth-century garment had been the *bliaut*, a floor-length tunic as worn by women, slightly shorter in the men's version. It was made of the costliest fabrics, oriental silks, satins, and velvets, and decorated with bands of embroidery, often with gold thread (*orfrois*, brocade). This elaborate court costume is worn on one ceremonial occasion in *Guillaume de Dole* when three noblemen carry Guillaume's shields in a procession.

The skirt of the women's *bliaut* was cut separately from the bodice and very full, with a train. It was long-waisted and close-fitting, often laced on the sides. A long silk cord, sometimes ornamented with gold and jewels, was wrapped twice around the figure, and in the thirteenth century was almost always equipped with a purse, called an *aumosniere* because its original use had been to carry coins for alms.

The sleeves of the *bliaut* were sometimes so long that they touched the ground. Goddard gives a late twelfth-century date for *Guillaume de Dole*, a generation earlier than most assessments, because the upper sleeves are still so full that the emperor has his held back when he washes his hands. It might be, however, that Conrad's costume, despite his egalitarian inclinations, was extreme in this regard, since the need for this service is not mentioned in the many other scenes in which hands are washed. Jean Renart's characters wore the lower sleeves so tight they had to be sewn on each time they were worn, a fashion only occasionally seen earlier. Ladies' maids carry sleeve-sewing equipment in their *aumosnieres*, and squires come running with thread before the tournament begins.

Ladies in *Guillaume de Dole* often wear the *chainse*, which had been a rather undistinguished relative of the *bliaut*. In Chrétien's *Erec and Enide*, Enide's *chainse*, a sign of her poverty, was replaced by a rich *bliaut*, given by the queen. The *chainse*, which we have translated as "tunic," was usually made of less elaborate, even washable, white material. (Quicherat and Enlart both tell us, however, that what is called "white" in the texts was actually a cream color, more highly regarded than blue-white and the result of saffron dye which also made it scented.) The *chainse* was simpler in design than the *bliaut* but could still be very elegant, for example those, pleated and tightly laced, worn at Conrad's summertime festivities. It could also have a train.

The principal characters in *Guillaume de Dole* wear the *cote* and, a new invention, the *sorcot*. The *cote* was originally the basic tunic with sleeves worn by men and women of all classes. In *Guillaume de Dole* it is sufficiently luxurious to be worn to court, as Liénor does. Hers was green cendal silk lined with fur. (According to Quicherat, *cendal* was a kind of taffeta.) Her *cote* is low-waisted, in accordance with the preference, constant in this whole period, for long, slender figures.

The *sorcot*, according to Goddard, appears at the end of the twelfth century; she notes that it is not found in the works of Marie de France, and only in the two later of Chrétien's romances. The *sorcot*, which could be edged with fur and made of rich fabric, was worn over the *cote*. Relying on details in the iconography rather than on the rather vague textual descriptions, Goddard defines it as a tunic without sleeves, or with half sleeves, so that the sleeves of the *cote* would be seen, contrasting in color. The *sorcot* seems to have hung straight down, but a belt was often worn over it. Guillaume, in his rooms at Saint-Trond, wears over his *chemise* a *sorcot* decorated on the back with English brocade, lined with scarlet silk, and trimmed with ermine. The neck opening of these various kinds of tunic was fastened with an elaborate gold and jeweled brooch. Buttons were available, either for this purpose or for fastening sleeves, but seem to be not much in favor.

A person fully dressed would always wear a *mantel* (cloak). This was the most sumptuous part of the costume, lined with fur in all seasons, and fastened with cords, usually of silk. The cloak Liénor wears to court is indigo samite lined with ermine. When she appears before the king, she "pulls the cloak away from her neck." This recurrent expression is always understood (with *Guillaume de Dole* as a principal reference) to mean that the cloak was removed in the presence of a person of higher rank. But since the cloak neither falls to the floor nor is handed to anyone, we wonder if it might not be simply pushed back off the shoulders and held by the cord.

In addition to the many varieties of fabric both imported and domestic, often vivid in color, medieval aristocratic dress required an astonishing amount of fur. Linings and edging might be made of ermine or sable; *vair*, the bluish-grey of squirrel fur; *gris*, the gray winter fur; *menu vair*, which became "miniver," the white belly fur alternating with the blue-gray in a variety of patterns.

Bliaut, *chainse*, and *cote* were worn over the *chemise* ("shift" for women, "shirt" for the somewhat shorter men's version), a long-sleeved undergarment made of soft fine fabric, sometimes pleated and sometimes laced on the sides. They could be elaborately embroidered, as was Liénor's when she went to court. Under the *chemise*, men wore *braies*, long, rather loose trousers. Both men and women wore *chausses*, stockings, of ordinary cloth or silk, held up by garters. Fashionable twelfth-century shoes had very long pointed toes, much complained about in sermons. By the time of *Guillaume de Dole* these would have been reduced in length and rounded.

In cold weather, a *peliçon* might be added to the costume. This was a garment which varied in cut, consisting of two layers of cloth with fur between them.

Other items of men's clothing mentioned in *Guillaume de Dole* are the *porpoint* and the *gamboison*, padded garments worn under the hauberk, a chain-mail coat. They seem to be ancestors of the "doublet" and there is at least one occasion when the *porpoint* is clearly an outer garment: Guillaume wears his covered with cloth-of-gold for an evening at the palace. Guillaume's clothing and even the trappings of his horses are embroidered with his arms, done in brocade; their high cost is often mentioned. (One wonders what the arms of a person "not from Dole" might have been.) In any event this fashion may be new. Quicherat quotes Joinville, who, at the beginning of the fourteenth century, reproached Philippe le Hardi for the extravagance of having his arms worked in gold thread instead of simply in silk as his father had done.

Men were clean-shaven and wore their hair long. Both men and women wore chaplets of flowers or circlets of jeweled gold. Liénor, going to court, covers her hair with an elaborate wimple. Lejeune notes how its description suggests various aspects of armor. When the headdress gets caught in her cloak and falls off, a chaplet, probably a plain metal band, still holds back her hair which is not braided but hangs in curls, whether naturally or otherwise.

To complete the costume, Jean Renart is very fond of white gloves and narrow white leather belts for both men and women, not only at parties but also as part of tournament attire.

Bibliographical Note

Our information on costume comes principally from the following sources, all of which frequently cite *Guillaume de Dole* as a source of their own information:

Enlart, Camille. *Manuel d'Archéologie française*, vol. III, *Le Costume*. Paris: Auguste Picard, 1916.

Goddard, Eunice Rathbone. *Women's Costume in French Texts of the Eleventh and Twelfth Centuries*. Baltimore: Johns Hopkins University Press, 1927.

Quicherat, Jules. *Histoire du costume en France*. Paris: Hachette, 1875.

Appendix 2

The following is a list of the first lines of songs included in *Guillaume de Dole*. Authors, when known, are indicated. For additional information, consult Lecoy's edition, pp. xxii–xxix.

1. p. 22
I swear to God! if I can't get
his love, I wish we'd never met.
(E non Deu, sire, se ne l'ai,
l'amor de lui, mar l'acointai.) ll. 291–92

2. p. 22
Under the branches bending low
(La jus, desoz la raime) ll. 295–99

3. p. 22
And if my love's abandoned me,
I will not die of that, you'll see!
(Se mes amis m'a guerpie,
por ce ne morrai ge mie.) ll. 304–5

4. p. 22
Lovely Aelis got up with the sun—
sleep well, I pray you, jealous one
(Main se leva bele Aeliz,
dormez, jalous, ge vos en pri) ll. 310–15

5. p. 22
Lovely Aelis got up with the day,
I see her come dancing along
(Main se leva bele Aeliz,
mignotement la voi venir) ll. 318–22

6. p. 23
Down there where flowers grow
(C'est tot la gieus, el glaioloi) ll. 329–33

7. p. 25
Away down there in the meadow
(C'est tot la gieus, enmi les prez) ll. 514–19

8. p. 25
Down there under the olive tree
(C'est la jus desoz l'olive) ll. 522–27

9. p. 25
Aelis got up with the sun—
I'm called Enmelot
(Main se levoit Aaliz,
J'ai non Enmelot.) ll. 532–37

10. p. 26
The beautiful Aelis gets up with the day.
Dark and handsome Robin is coming her way.
(Main se leva la bien fete Aeliz,
par ci passe li bruns, li biaus Robins.) ll. 542–47

11. p. 29
When flowers and leaves and grasses fade away
(Quant flors et glais et verdure s'esloigne) ll. 846–52
Gace Brulé

12. p. 30
The violets blooming once again in May
(Li noviaus tens et mais [et violete]) ll. 923–30
Châtelain de Couci

13. p. 33
A mother and daughter sit and sew
(Fille et la mere se sieent a l'orfrois) ll. 1159–66

14. p. 33
Lovely Aye sits at a cruel lady's feet
(Siet soi bele Aye as piez sa male maistre) ll. 1183–92

15. p. 34
Lovely Doette, where breezes blow
(La bele Doe siet au vent) ll. 1203–16

16. p. 36
When the days grow long in May
(Lors que li jor sont lonc en mai) ll. 1301–07
Jaufré Rudel

17. p. 36
When Fromont insulted the Hunter
(Des que Fromonz au Veneor tença) ll. 1335–67
A fragment of epic from the *Gerbert de Metz* story.

18. p. 38
When true love dwells within a heart that's pure
(Loial amor qui en fin cuer s'est mise) ll. 1456–69
Renaut de Beaujeu

19. p. 40
Aelis arose very early—
Greetings to her with all my heart!
(Aaliz main se leva.
Bon jor ait qui mon cuer a!) ll. 1579–84

20. p. 42
It's been so long
since I last heard
(Mout me demeure
que n'oi chanter) ll. 1769–76

21. p. 44
Perronele was in the meadow
(C'est la jus en la praele) ll. 1846–51

22. p. 46
In this bitter time of the year
(Contrel tens que voi frimer) ll. 2027–35
Gace Brulé

23. p. 49
In a royal chamber, beautiful Eglantine
(Bele Aiglentine en roial chamberine) ll. 2235–94

24. p. 51
Where the olive tree bends low
(La jus desouz l'olive) ll. 2369–74

25. p. 51
Mauberjon got up early today
(Mauberjon s'est main levee) ll. 2379–85

26. p. 52
Across a field Renaut rides with his lady
(Renaus et s'amie chevauche par un pré) ll. 2389–91

27. p. 52
Of Renaut of Mousson
(De Renaut de Moussonet) ll. 2398–2404

28. p. 53
Under the branches bending low
(La gieus desoz la raime) ll. 2514–18

29. p. 54
To the shore of the sea
(Sor la rive de mer) ll. 2523–27

30. p. 61
Whatever they say, it's madness
(Mout est fouls, que que nus die) ll. 3107–14

31. p. 62
When the orchard trees are once again in leaf
(Quant de la foelle espoissent li vergier) ll. 3180–87

32. p. 65
I gave her the white fur-lined vest
(Quant ge li donai le blanc peliçon) ll. 3403–06

33. p. 65
She's from Oissery
and never forgets
(Cele d'Oisseri
ne met en oubli) ll. 3419–30

34. p. 67
You're out of your mind
(Je di que c'est granz folie) ll. 3625–31
Gace Brulé

35. p. 69
Tell me for what reason or what crime
(Por quel forfet ne por quel ochoison) ll. 3751–59
Châtelain de Couci or Roger d'Andeli

36. p. 71
Now I shall sing no more
(Ja de chanter en ma vie) ll. 3883–98
Renaut (or Robert) de Sabloeil

37. p. 74
When we have once again enjoyed the spring
(Quant la sesons del douz tens s'asseüre) ll. 4127–40

38. p. 75
Down there by the sea
(Tout la gieus, sor rive mer) ll. 4164–69

39. p. 80
When it's the season
(Quant revient la sesons) l. 4568–83

40. p. 80
This suffering, this torment—love is its name
(Amours a non ciz maus qui me tormente) ll. 4587–93

41. p. 81
I delight to hear the lofty voice
(Bele m'est la voiz altane) ll. 4653–59
Daude de Pradas

42. p. 86
What more do you want,
when I am yours?
(Que demandez vos
quant vos m'avez?) ll. 5106–11

43. p. 87
Hold out your hands for the summer flowers
(Tendez tuit voz mains a la flor d'esté) ll. 5113–15

44. p. 88
Now that April's beauty can be seen
(Or vienent Pasques les beles en avril) ll. 5188–5207

45. p. 88
When I see a lark on the wing
(Quant voi l'aloete moder) ll. 5212–27
Bernart de Ventadorn

46. p. 89
When the heather blooms in spring
(Lors que florist la bruiere) ll. 5232–52
Gontier de Soignies

47. p. 91
Down there, down there in the meadow, they say
(C'est la gieus, la gieus, q'en dit en ces prez) ll. 5427–34

48. p. 92
Down there in the meadow
(C'est la gieus, en mi les prez) ll. 5440–45

Selected Bibliography

Baldwin, John W. "Jean Renart et le tournoi de Saint-Trond: une conjonction de l'histoire et de la littérature." *Annales ESC* 3 (1990): 565–88.

———. "Five Discourses on Desire: Sexuality and Gender in Northern France Around 1200." *Speculum* 66.4 (1991): 797–819.

Coldwell, Maria V. "*Guillaume de Dole* and Medieval Romances with Musical Interpolations." *Musica Disciplina* 35 (1981): 55–86.

de Looze, Laurence. "The Gender of Fiction: Womanly Poetics in Jean Renart's *Guillaume de Dole*." *French Review* 64.4 (1991): 596–606.

Diller, George T. "Remarques sur la structure esthétique du *Guillaume de Dole*." *Romania* 98 (1977): 390–98.

———. "Techniques de contraste dans *Guillaume de Dole*." *Romania* 99 (1978): 538–49.

Dragonetti, Roger. *Le Mirage des sources: l'art du faux dans le roman médiéval.* Paris: Seuil, 1987.

Dufournet, Jean, Jacques Kooijman, René Menage, and Christine Tronc, trans. *Guillaume de Dole ou Le Roman de la Rose.* Second edition. Paris: Champion, 1988.

Durling, Nancy Vine. "The Seal and the Rose: Erotic Exchanges in *Guillaume de Dole*." *Neophilologus* 77 (1993): 31–40.

Fourrier, Anthime. "Les Armoiries de l'empereur dans *Guillaume de Dole*." *Mélanges Offerts à Rita Lejeune*, vol. 2. Gembloux: Édition J. Duculot, 1969. 1211–26.

Huot, Sylvia. *From Song to Book: The Poetics of Writing in Old French Lyric and Lyrical Narrative Poetry.* Ithaca and London: Cornell University Press, 1987.

Jung, Marc-René. "L'Empereur Conrad, chanteur de poésie lyrique." *Romania* 101 (1980): 35–50.

Kay, Sarah. *Subjectivity in Troubadour Lyric.* Cambridge: Cambridge University Press, 1990.

Lacy, Norris. "'Amer par oïr dire': *Guillaume de Dole* and the Drama of Language." *French Review* 54.6 (1981): 779–87.

Lecoy, Félix. "Sur quelques passages difficiles du *Guillaume de Dole*." *Romania* 82 (1961): 244–60.

———, ed. *Jean Renart: Le Roman de la Rose ou de Guillaume de Dole.* Paris: Champion [Classiques Français du Moyen Age], 1979.

Lejeune, Rita, ed. *Jean Renart: Le Roman de la Rose ou de Guillaume de Dole.* Paris: Droz, 1936.

Lejeune-Dehousse, Rita. *L'Oeuvre de Jean Renart.* Paris: Droz, 1935.

Page, Christopher. *The Owl and the Nightingale: Musical Life and Ideas in France 1100–1300.* Berkeley and Los Angeles: University of California Press, 1989.

―――. *Voices and Instruments in the Middle Ages: Instrumental Practice and Songs in France 1100–1300*. Berkeley and Los Angeles: University of California Press: 1986.

Régnier-Bohler, Danielle. "Imagining the Self." In *A History of Private Life: II. Revelations of the Medieval World*. Ed. Georges Duby. Trans. Arthur Goldhammer. Cambridge, Mass. and London: Belknap Press of Harvard University Press, 1988.

Rey-Flaud, Henri. *La Névrose courtoise*. Seuil: Navarin, 1983.

Servois, G., ed. *Le Roman de la Rose ou de Guillaume de Dole*. Paris: Firmin Didot, 1893.

Zink, Michel. *Roman Rose et Rose Rouge: Le Roman de la Rose ou de Guillaume de Dole de Jean Renart*. Paris: Nizet, 1979.

Index of Historical Personages

University of Pennsylvania Press
MIDDLE AGES SERIES
Edward Peters, General Editor

F. R. P. Akehurst, trans. *The* Coutumes de Beauvaisis *of Philippe de Beaumanoir.* 1992
Peter Allen. *The Art of Love: Amatory Fiction from Ovid to the* Romance of the Rose. 1992
David Anderson. *Before the Knight's Tale: Imitation of Classical Epic in Boccaccio's* Teseida. 1988
Benjamin Arnold. *Count and Bishop in Medieval Germany: A Study of Regional Power, 1100–1350.* 1991
Mark C. Bartusis. *The Late Byzantine Army: Arms and Society, 1204–1453.* 1992
J. M. W. Bean. *From Lord to Patron: Lordship in Late Medieval England.* 1990
Uta-Renate Blumenthal. *The Investiture Controversy: Church and Monarchy from the Ninth to the Twelfth Century.* 1988
Daniel Bornstein, trans. *Dino Compagni's* Chronicle *of Florence.* 1986
Maureen Barry McCann Boulton. *The Song in the Story: Lyric Insertions in French Narrative Fiction, 1200–1400.* 1993.
Betsy Bowden. *Chaucer Aloud: The Varieties of Textual Interpretation.* 1987
James William Brodman. *Ransoming Captives in Crusader Spain: The Order of Merced on the Christian-Islamic Frontier.* 1986
Kevin Brownlee and Sylvia Huot. *Rethinking the* Romance of the Rose*: Text, Image, Reception.* 1992
Matilda Tomaryn Bruckner. *Shaping Romance: Truth and Closure in Twelfth-Century French Fictions.* 1993.
Otto Brunner (Howard Kaminsky and James Van Horn Melton, eds. and trans.). Land *and Lordship: Structures of Governance in Medieval Austria.* 1992
Robert I. Burns, S.J., ed. *Emperor of Culture: Alfonso X the Learned of Castile and His Thirteenth-Century Renaissance.* 1990
David Burr. *Olivi and Franciscan Poverty: The Origins of the* Usus Pauper *Controversy.* 1989
David Burr. *Peaceable Kingdom: A Reading of Olivi's Apocalypse Commentary.* 1993
Thomas Cable. *The English Alliterative Tradition.* 1991
Anthony K. Cassell and Victoria Kirkham, eds. and trans. *Diana's Hunt / Caccia di Diana: Boccaccio's First Fiction.* 1991
John C. Cavadini. *The Last Christology of the West: Adoptionism in Spain and Gaul, 785–820.* 1993
Brigitte Cazelles. *The Lady as Saint: A Collection of French Hagiographic Romances of the Thirteenth Century.* 1991
Karen Cherewatuk and Ulrike Wiethaus, eds. *Dear Sister: Medieval Women and the Epistolary Genre.* 1993

Anne L. Clark. *Elisabeth of Schönau: A Twelfth-Century Visionary.* 1992

Willene B. Clark and Meradith T. McMunn, eds. *Beasts and Birds of the Middle Ages: The Bestiary and Its Legacy.* 1989

Richard C. Dales. *The Scientific Achievement of the Middle Ages.* 1973

Charles T. Davis. *Dante's Italy and Other Essays.* 1984

Katherine Fischer Drew, trans. *The Burgundian Code.* 1972

Katherine Fischer Drew, trans. *The Laws of the Salian Franks.* 1991

Katherine Fischer Drew, trans. *The Lombard Laws.* 1973

Nancy Edwards. *The Archaeology of Early Medieval Ireland.* 1990

Margaret J. Ehrhart. *The Judgment of the Trojan Prince Paris in Medieval Literature.* 1987

Richard K. Emmerson and Ronald B. Herzman. *The Apocalyptic Imagination in Medieval Literature.* 1992

Theodore Evergates. *Feudal Society in Medieval France: Documents from the County of Champagne.* 1993

Felipe Fernández-Armesto. *Before Columbus: Exploration and Colonization from the Mediterranean to the Atlantic, 1229–1492.* 1987

Robert D. Fulk. *A History of Old English Meter.* 1992

Patrick J. Geary. *Aristocracy in Provence: The Rhône Basin at the Dawn of the Carolingian Age.* 1985

Peter Heath. *Allegory and Philosophy in Avicenna (Ibn Sînâ), With a Translation of the Book of the Prophet Muḥammad's Ascent to Heaven.* 1992

J. N. Hillgarth, ed. *Christianity and Paganism, 350–750: The Conversion of Western Europe.* 1986

Richard C. Hoffmann. *Land, Liberties, and Lordship in a Late Medieval Countryside: Agrarian Structures and Change in the Duchy of Wrocław.* 1990

Robert Hollander. *Boccaccio's Last Fiction: Il Corbaccio.* 1988

Edward B. Irving, Jr. *Rereading* Beowulf. 1989

C. Stephen Jaeger. *The Origins of Courtliness: Civilizing Trends and the Formation of Courtly Ideals, 939–1210.* 1985

William Chester Jordan. *The French Monarchy and the Jews: From Philip Augustus to the Last Capetians.* 1989

William Chester Jordan. *From Servitude to Freedom: Manumission in the Sénonais in the Thirteenth Century.* 1986

Ellen E. Kittell. *From Ad Hoc to Routine: A Case Study in Medieval Bureaucracy.* 1991

Alan C. Kors and Edward Peters, eds. *Witchcraft in Europe, 1100–1700: A Documentary History.* 1972

Barbara M. Kreutz. *Before the Normans: Southern Italy in the Ninth and Tenth Centuries.* 1992

E. Ann Matter. *The Voice of My Beloved: The Song of Songs in Western Medieval Christianity.* 1990

María Rosa Menocal. *The Arabic Role in Medieval Literary History.* 1987

A. J. Minnis. *Medieval Theory of Authorship.* 1988

Lawrence Nees. *A Tainted Mantle: Hercules and the Classical Tradition at the Carolingian Court.* 1991

Lynn H. Nelson, trans. *The Chronicle of San Juan de la Peña: A Fourteenth-Century Official History of the Crown of Aragon.* 1991

Charlotte A. Newman. *The Anglo-Norman Nobility in the Reign of Henry I: The Second Generation.* 1988

Joseph F. O'Callaghan. *The Cortes of Castile-León, 1188–1350.* 1989

Joseph F. O'Callaghan. *The Learned King: The Reign of Alfonso X of Castile.* 1993

William D. Paden, ed. *The Voice of the Trobairitz: Perspectives on the Women Troubadours.* 1989

Edward Peters. *The Magician, the Witch, and the Law.* 1982

Edward Peters, ed. *Christian Society and the Crusades, 1198–1229: Sources in Translation, including The* Capture of Damietta *by Oliver of Paderborn.* 1971

Edward Peters, ed. *The First Crusade: The* Chronicle of Fulcher of Chartres *and Other Source Materials.* 1971

Edward Peters, ed. *Heresy and Authority in Medieval Europe.* 1980

James M. Powell. *Albertanus of Brescia: The Pursuit of Happiness in the Early Thirteenth Century.* 1992

James M. Powell. *Anatomy of a Crusade, 1213–1221.* 1986

Jean Renart. (Patricia Terry and Nancy Vine Durling, trans.) *The Romance of the Rose or Guillaume de Dole.* 1993

Michael Resler, trans. Erec *by Hartmann von Aue.* 1987

Pierre Riché (Michael Idomir Allen, trans.). *The Carolingians: A Family Who Forged Europe.* 1993

Pierre Riché (Jo Ann McNamara, trans.). *Daily Life in the World of Charlemagne.* 1978

Jonathan Riley-Smith. *The First Crusade and the Idea of Crusading.* 1986

Joel T. Rosenthal. *Patriarchy and Families of Privilege in Fifteenth-Century England.* 1991

Teofilo F. Ruiz. *Crisis and Continuity: The Urban and Rural Structures of Late Medieval Castile.* 1993

Steven D. Sargent, ed. and trans. *On the Threshold of Exact Science: Selected Writings of Anneliese Maier on Late Medieval Natural Philosophy.* 1982

Sarah Stanbury. *Seeing the* Gawain-Poet: Description and the Act of Perception. 1992

Thomas C. Stillinger. *The Song of Troilus: Lyric Authority in the Medieval Book.* 1992

Susan Mosher Stuard. *A State of Deference: Ragusa/Dubrovnik in the Medieval Centuries.* 1992

Susan Mosher Stuard, ed. *Women in Medieval History and Historiography.* 1987

Susan Mosher Stuard, ed. *Women in Medieval Society.* 1976

Jonathan Sumption. *The Hundred Years War: Trial by Battle.* 1992

Ronald E. Surtz. *The Guitar of God: Gender, Power, and Authority in the Visionary World of Mother Juana de la Cruz (1481–1534).* 1990

Patricia Terry, trans. *Poems of the Elder Edda.* 1990

Hugh M. Thomas. *Vassals, Heiresses, Crusaders, and Thugs: The Gentry of Angevin Yorkshire, 1154–1216.* 1993

Frank Tobin. *Meister Eckhart: Thought and Language.* 1986

Ralph V. Turner. *Men Raised from the Dust: Administrative Service and Upward Mobility in Angevin England.* 1988

Harry Turtledove, trans. *The* Chronicle of Theophanes: An English Translation of Anni Mundi 6095–6305 (A.D. 602–813). 1982

Mary F. Wack. *Lovesickness in the Middle Ages: The* Viaticum *and Its Commentaries.* 1990

Benedicta Ward. *Miracles and the Medieval Mind: Theory, Record, and Event, 1000–1215.* 1982

Suzanne Fonay Wemple. *Women in Frankish Society: Marriage and the Cloister, 500–900.* 1981

Jan M. Ziolkowski. *Talking Animals: Medieval Latin Beast Poetry, A.D. 750–1150.* 1993

This book has been set in Linotron Galliard. Galliard was designed for Mergenthaler in 1978 by Matthew Carter. Galliard retains many of the features of a sixteenth-century typeface cut by Robert Granjon but has some modifications that give it a more contemporary look.

Printed on acid-free paper.